Stocks and Shares Simplified

A GUIDE FOR THE SMALLER INVESTOR

Second Edition

Stocks and Shares Simplified

A GUIDE FOR THE SMALLER INVESTOR

Second Edition

BRIAN J. MILLARD

JOHN WILEY & SONS LTD
Chichester · New York · Brisbane · Toronto · Singapore

Library of Congress Cataloging-in-Publication Data:

Millard, Brian J.
    Stocks and shares simplified.

    Includes index.
    1. Speculation.   2. Stocks.   3.Investments.
I. Title.
HG6041.M52   1986   332.6'78   85-22767

ISBN 0 471 90910 6

British Library Cataloguing in Publication Data:

Millard, Brian J.
    Stocks and shares simplified: a guide for the
    smaller investor.—2nd ed.
    1. Securities   2. Stocks
    I. Title
    332.63'22   HG4521

ISBN 0 471 90910 6

Typeset by Mathematical Composition Setters Ltd, Salisbury, UK
Printed and bound in Great Britain

Contents

Preface

It is nearly five years since the first edition of *Stocks and Shares Simplified* was published. These five years have been probably the most significant and eventful ever in the history of the UK investment scene.

We have seen inflation come down from over 20% to somewhere around 5%, so that investors now have a positive rather than a negative return on their investments, and the capital gains to be made by successful stock market investing become even more valuable.

We have seen the market itself, as measured by the *Financial Times* Index, move to over the 1000 mark during the first half of 1985, while the highest point it had reached by the publication date of the first edition was 558.6 in May 1979. Investors who followed the principles outlined in *Stocks and Shares Simplified* have had an extremely profitable five years, and should at least have doubled their money. Many will have performed even better than this.

We have seen the introduction of a new index for measuring the market, the *Financial Times* Stock Exchange 100 Index, called the FTSE-100 index, which gives us a broader measure of the market than the FT30 Index.

We have seen the enormous growth in the use of microcomputers in home and business spill over into the investment scene, with many programs now available to store and retrieve stock market prices and perform complex analyses on these. All calculations of moving averages, etc., used in this book have been carried out on popular microcomputers, and many of the diagrams have also been produced by this means. The availability of share prices at all times of the day on your TV screen via Prestel, Ceefax and Oracle and the recent availability at reasonable cost of price data down the telephone line to your computer, plus the ability to place orders with a stockbroker through a home terminal has kept investors well to the forefront of the high technology revolution.

From an investment author's point of view, the most important development, has been the tremendous increase in awareness of the Stock Market, and in the number of investors in the UK. This has come about as the result of Government policy on privatization, the British Telecom launch being responsible for the creation of nearly two million first-time shareholders. Recent estimates now put the number of UK investors who own shares directly at over three million.

The first edition of this book made the point that, contrary to popular opinion, it was not necessary to have a great deal of money in order to venture into stock market investment. Even today, I still see, in literature at the counters of the major clearing banks, that sums of the order of £20 000 are necessary before undertaking investment in the stock market. This is absolute nonsense, and the recent launch of British Telecom has underlined this fact, since the vast majority of investors applied for amounts of shares costing much less than a thousand pounds well before government policy on the allocation of these shares was known.

Even though potential investors can now see that large sums of money are not necessary in order to enter the stock market, many of them will feel that there are two further aspects which hold them back. They think that there is a great deal of risk involved in buying and selling shares, and they also think that a vast amount of time is required to read the City pages of their newspapers in order to understand the workings of the market and so make a profit. There is risk involved in stock market investment, and there is no doubt that many first-time investors in British Telecom do not appreciate this point. The value of their shares will go down as well as up over the course of time. The main purpose of this book is to show that, compared with haphazard buying and selling decisions, based on newspaper tips, overheard snippets of conversation, advice from persons not qualified to give such advice, etc., a logical approach to stock market investment can substantially reduce the risks involved. A logical approach will also reduce the amount of time needed to manage your investments, turning what can be a chore into a source of enjoyment.

Investment in the stock market requires you to make only three important decisions—What to buy; When to buy it; When to sell it. A way is shown, which has proved successful in the past, of picking just a handful of shares from the many thousands of shares quoted. The book concentrates on ways in which the investor can judge the correct time to buy, and then sell these shares, so that he or she can avoid the pitfall of buying at the top of the price range and selling at the bottom.

YOU should be the best person to look after YOUR investments, and by the time you have finished this book, you will be.

May 1985   Brian J. Millard
                                                  Weston Turville

Chapter 1

Introduction

It is an oddity of the British Press that stock market and financial information is to be found towards the back of your newspaper, fairly close to the sports pages, and usually running into the horse racing results. It might be that many editors feel that there is not much difference between investing in the stock market and placing a bet on a horse in the 3 o'clock at Kempton! In some circumstances they may have a point, since investment in the market at the wrong time, just like placing a bet on the wrong horse, will inevitably lead to losses in your investment. Another interesting analogy between the stock market and racing is that they both suffer from the activities of the 'insider', who knows exactly what is going on well before anybody else wakes up to the fact.

While not wishing to proceed too far with sporting analogies, we can get rather more insight into the workings of the stock market by looking at it, for a moment, as if it is some sort of game. The stock market game is, like most games, between two sides, which in this case are on the one hand the buyers, and on the other hand, the sellers.

Most games, quite reasonably, take place between sides which are, at least at the start of play, evenly balanced in numbers, if not in skill at playing the game. The stock market game is quite different, since besides involving players of quite different levels of skill, the *numbers* of players on each side are constantly changing. We have the option of joining one side or the other, and of changing sides at any time if we judge our side to be losing— we may be a buyer today and a seller tomorrow. We have virtually the freedom of choice of the small boy who actually owns the football used in a kick-around in the local park. This battle has been going on for hundreds of years and will continue to do so as long as there is a stock market. There will never be an outright winning side in this game; one may gain a temporary advantage, but as surely as night follows day, this advantage will

1

move to the other side. Since, of course, the individual player can change sides, he or she can be a winner or loser in this game. The winner will see a steady gain in the value of his capital, while the loser will see his money trickle or even flood away.

The investor who has yet to make up his mind as to which side to join is like a spectator at this game. The uninformed investor will naturally assume that the side with the most players is going to win, and so when investors are clamouring to buy shares he will join their ranks. The informed investor, on the other hand, may well spot that some of the players are looking a little jaded and that the other side could well come out on top, until once more he can read the signs that the buying side is about to come into its own and then join them.

The whole philosophy about stock market investment is to be ahead of the majority in your thinking and not to join the crowd when the game is poised to swing the other way. Therein lies the key to consistent profits, year after year. The reader may feel that this is a very easy statement to make, but which is difficult to attain in practice. However, success can be achieved if a few basic principles are accepted. We have said that the advantage constantly switches from buyers to sellers, which means that prices go up and prices come down over the course of time. If we assume that stock market prices are not totally random, then a moment's thought should convince you that the longer the time for which prices have been rising, the greater is the chance that they will start to fall. It seems to be a fact of life that the majority think in the opposite way, i.e. that when prices have been rising for some considerable time, then they will continue to do so, and it is sensible to invest even more in the market. By applying the principles discussed in this book, you will be able to put yourself in the former category of those who are ahead of the majority in your buying and selling operations.

Besides thinking that he can see which way the game is going, what makes a person a buyer or a seller? The answer essentially can be boiled down to two emotions: greed and fear. Fear of further losses drives some people to sell their holdings, while greed, the desire to make a large profit, sends people to the market as buyers. So, in a sense, the battle in the stock market is a fight between greed and fear. As with other emotions, these two can be destructive in the sense that they blind one to the obvious and also that they are contagious. It is difficult to reason with a crowd motivated by fear or greed, and the herd instinct is strong. It takes courage not to join the lemmings, but this courage must not be of the blind sort—it must be based on an understanding of the facts. After all, the crowd is occasionally right! It is instructive to look at some of the charts of the FT Index in Chapter 5 for the year 1974 to see the effect of fear on the market. The investor taking a logical approach would have been rubbing his hands with glee in the certainty that the market had to change direction. His glee would have been well-founded, because within a few short months after reaching the bottom the FT Index had doubled, and many shares had even tripled in value.

The key to successful investing is an ability to stand apart from fear and greed and other emotions and to base one's investment posture on a reading of the signals which the market is giving. This is easier said than done. When a share which you have bought has risen in value by, say, some 50%, then there is a psychological barrier to selling, since one expects the share to go on rising. A failure to take a firmly objective view of the situation can result in riding the share down to zero profit again, and perhaps even turning the profit into a loss. There are many old adages doing the rounds of the investment scene, for example 'any profit is a good profit' and 'cut your losses and let your profits run'. The first one should be replaced with 'a large profit is better than a small profit', since there is nothing more frustrating than to sell a holding when the bulk of the profit is still to come. As far as the second adage is concerned, many investors, through the temptation to 'wait a little longer' in the hope that their buying situation will prove correct, let their losses run. We should all take the view that 'a small loss is better than a large loss'. It is true to say, however, that correct selling is the most difficult aspect of stock market investment. A failure to sell at the right time can be due to various psychological difficulties—greed, a desire to be proved right, the need to avoid admitting failure, etc. Of course, there are many occasions when it is wrong to sell, and by selling, a large potential profit is missed. In this case the problem is often one of worry about the degree of commitment to the particular security. Since, of course, you do need to sleep well at night, the best course of action in such a situation is to sell a part, rather than all, of the holding in that security to bring it down to a level at which you feel more comfortable.

Risk is an integral part of investment and there is no doubt that the stock market is a place of greater risk than a bank deposit account or building society account. Risk can be said to be dependent mainly upon two major factors. The first of these is the quality of the equity chosen for investment, which is tied to its volatility or historical price fluctuation. Classical investment theory equates the degree of risk with the volatility of a share. The greater the volatility, the greater the risk in investing in that share. However, this statement ignores the second important factor in investment in the stock market, which is timing. There is no doubt that a volatile share, chosen at a random point in time, has a potential for greater loss than a relatively non-volatile share. Of course, it also has a potential for a larger gain. The whole point is that, in the absence of timing, investment in a very volatile share is a large gamble. Of course, under such random conditions investment in a less volatile share is also a gamble, albeit a lesser one. Note, however, that whatever the share, a gamble is still involved if no notice is taken whatsoever of correct timing, both from the point of view of general market conditions and in terms of the history of a particular share. So the most important factor in decreasing risk is buying at the correct time. Proper timing minimizes the risk not only for non-volatile shares but for volatile ones as well. Since risk is minimized, it will make sense to invest in volatile shares since these hold out the prospect of larger gains.

In this book we are going to develop a method of correct timing of buying operations by attempting to locate major low points in the market as a whole. From such low points the majority of equities increase in value and so low risk is associated with such low points in the market.

Once a security has been bought at a time of low risk, that, of course, is not the end of the matter. Eventually there comes a time when the risk inherent in continued holding of the security becomes unacceptable and safety dictates that it should be sold. In this case, not only does the general state of the market become important, but also the behaviour of the security itself. Sometimes a particular share will top out with the rest of the market, and sometimes it reaches its high point before or after the market as a whole. After all, it is more correct to describe the market as a market of stocks rather than a stock market. Correct timing of a sale therefore depends upon the behaviour of the particular equity, and ways will be discussed of timing such sales.

Correct timing of investment buying and selling is only half of the investment story, the other half being a decision as to which securities should be bought. As already mentioned, volatility is a desirable feature since, if handled correctly, greater profits will ensue. The problem is that not all shares which were volatile last year will necessarily be performing well this year when the market takes off from a low point; in fact, they may well be volatile in a downward sense! A criterion used in this book is to choose from a long list of the most volatile shares, those which did not retreat as much during the last few months of the decline in the market to the low point we are establishing by our timing techniques. These can be considered to be relatively 'strong' shares and might be expected to lead the advance in the market, at least initially.

As in any other discipline, theories which are being put forward must stand up to the test of being put into practice. The techniques put forward in this book have in the past led to consistently higher profits than either random timings of random share selections, or even of correct timing in the 'blue chip' companies (considered by the market to be first-class investments) such as the constituents of the Financial Times 30 Index. Since history teaches us that the past gives us some guide to the future, then as far as stock market investment is concerned, a system which has worked well in the past may be expected to do the same in the future. It is not guaranteed to work, since nothing about the stock market is predictable with 100% certainty, but it will be stacking the odds in our favour. Success is virtually assured if we are right more times than we are wrong, but do not restrict our gains when we are right.

Chapter 2

Popular Forms of Investment

The stock market as a place for making money has to be judged against other forms of investment, taking into consideration several factors which are of prime importance whichever form of investment is followed. The various factors will have differing degrees of importance depending upon the personality and requirements of the particular investor. The most important ones are as follows:

1. *Return on the investment*—the income obtained plus any capital appreciation occurring during the period of the investment.
2. *Risk involved*—the degree of certainty that one can eventually withdraw one's money intact, together with any return on the investment.
3. *Liquidity*—the ability to withdraw one's money at short notice if unforeseen circumstances demand it.
4. *Time*—the amount of time needed personally to gain the necessary knowledge to make a wise investment and keep a vigilant eye on its progress.
5. *Tax*—one's personal tax position. Some investments have already had the tax on the interest deducted, and this may be non-returnable. Such a situation is better for a person in a high tax bracket than one paying little or no income tax. It should be noted that the tax on interest earned through an investment is much higher then the tax on capital gains, the first £6300 of which is tax-free (1985/6 budget).

Obviously the ideal investment would have a high return, high liquidity, low risk and attract the minimum tax, as well as taking minimal time to manage. Life being what it is, of course, it is not possible to obtain all of these things in one investment situation and a degree of trade-off of one factor against another has to be accepted, as also has a degree of diversification into other forms of investment.

6

The distinction between *investment* and *savings* is rather blurred. The term *savings* usually implies the money which has accrued from the frequent deposit of rather small sums, and which usually has attracted interest. *Investment* simply means the employing of money with the intention of making a profit, so that savings are one form of investment. The most popular forms of investment at the moment are the following:

Building Society Deposits. At the time of writing the interest paid is typically 8.25% if 7 days' notice of withdrawal is accepted. This has tax already deducted and not reclaimable, and is equivalent to 11.79% per annum for taxpayers at the 30% level. Slightly less interest is obtained for immediate withdrawal, and slightly more where societies operate 90-day schemes. The penalty for immediate withdrawal in such schemes is usually the loss of 90 days interest. This form of investment is suitable for regular savings or the deposit of larger sums of money.
Clearing Bank Deposits. The interest rate of the big four clearing banks is about 6.25% per annum, and tax is not deducted at source. Improved rates can be obtained with longer-term accounts, for example 9.75% for a 3-month term. This medium is also suitable for regular small deposits.
National Saving Certificate. For the 29th issue the rate is 6.0% for 1 year up to 8.0% for 5 years, tax free.
National Savings Investment Account. The interest rate at the time of writing is 11.25%, without deduction of tax.
Local Authority Bonds. Depending upon the local authority involved, interest rates at the time of writing run from 10.0% to 10.75%. The fixed term of deposit varies from 1 to 5 years, and minimum deposits are typically £500.

The returns from the above investment vehicles are constantly changing, but the latest rates, plus calculations of their pre-tax equivalents, are published in the financial sections of the Saturday and Sunday editions of the quality newspapers.

In all the above forms of investment, £1 invested is always worth £1 and the risk that the pound cannot be withdrawn on demand, or with the proper notice, is minute. Indeed, one can take the view that one's investment would only be affected by a catastrophe of such proportions that the value of money itself would be called into question. Except for local authority bonds, liquidity is high even though in some circumstances there may be a substantial penalty for early withdrawal. Demands on the investor's time are virtually zero and no specialized knowledge is necessary. Any change in interest rates is always recorded (in fact, frequently predicted!) in the press and, as mentioned above, the financial pages of the quality newspapers provide valuable comparisons of the relative returns amongst the forms of investment listed above.

The major disadvantage of all the above forms of investment has been that during periods of high inflation, such as during the period 1976 to 1982, the yield to the standard taxpayer has not been sufficient to keep up with inflation. The return has therefore been negative in real terms. The situation has improved over the past 2 years, and once again a positive return is obtained; nevertheless, the prospect is there that inflation may start to increase again. Two main options are open to an investor who wishes to achieve a capital growth sufficient to outweigh the ravages of inflation: either to invest in collectors' items, or to enter the stock market. However, unlike the previous types of investment, we will be considering situations in which £1 invested may result in the return of £5 or 20p. In other words there is a degree of risk involved which was not applicable to the foregoing forms of investment.

COLLECTORS' ITEMS

Collectors are willing to pay money for an astonishing variety of items, such as antiques, banknotes, coins, early radios, old cars, paintings, porcelain, postage stamps, railway bric-à-brac, sculptures etc. It is claimed that the three most popular collectors' items are stamps, coins and old postcards. The latter is perhaps surprising, but many cards originally costing 3d now change hands for £5, while rarer examples can fetch as much as £1500. It is possible to pick up bargains from market stalls if you know what you are looking for, but to be really successful with this form of investment a great deal of knowledge is necessary, which can only be obtained by a lot of time and effort. Many collectors of course get much value from admiring their collections, and the monetary aspect becomes secondary.

The best advice is to become familiar with some small area and purchase items which are in first-class condition, are in short supply and for which there is likely to be a demand in the not-too-distant future. As an example of what can be achieved, and in this case without too much effort, original gramophone records of rock and roll stars of the 1950s, which sold for between 25 and 50p at the time, now change hands for anything up to £150 or so.

Besides the need to become well-informed about the chosen sector of the market, there are two other obvious disadvantages to this method of investment. Firstly, with a few exceptions, a fairly long time-scale is involved if considerable gain are to be made—periods of 5 years and upwards. Secondly, it may be difficult to liquidate one's investment rapidly if the chosen area is highly specialized. In coin and stamp collecting this is not a particular problem, but it should be noted that the values quoted in catalogues from the specialist firms are always on the optimistic side and are rarely realized in practice. There is a lot to be said for investing in good wine, on the grounds that even if the market collapses, there is a lot of pleasure to be had from actually drinking your investment!

THE STOCK MARKET

A stock exchange deals in securities, which are of two types. On the London Stock Exchange about one-third of the securities are fixed-interest stocks, issued mainly by the Government (these are called 'gilt-edged' or 'gilts') but also by some companies (these are called debentures, loans and preference shares). The other two-thirds are the shares—called equities or ordinary shares—issued by companies. Stocks and shares are traded at prices which constantly vary, depending upon the buying and selling pressure upon that particular security, just as in any other market. While, as stated, stocks are fixed-interest, the dividend paid on an ordinary share can and usually does vary from year to year. Sometimes no dividend may be paid for several years if the particular company is going through a bad patch. Such is the variety of securities obtainable on the Stock Exchange that degrees of risk from very low to very high exist, depending on the security. They can satisfy the needs of the Church Commissioners or an outright gambler. Investors can buy a security with a projected long-term growth but low yield, or the security of a virtually static company which regularly pays out high dividends. It is usual to spread the risk by investing in several securities (a 'portfolio') including both growth and high-income shares, as well as some gilt-edged.

Stock Exchange securities have the advantage of high liquidity and they can be bought or sold on any day that the Stock Exchange is open but payment is neither required nor received until after the end of an account period, which is usually of 2 weeks' duration. Securities can be bought either through one's bank or by using a broker.

UNIT TRUSTS

A simple way for the small investor to enter the Stock Market is by buying units in a unit trust. Unit trusts have a spread of investments which is divided into equal units. The buying and selling prices are usually called 'bid' and 'offer' prices. The latter is slightly higher than the former, for example Save & Prosper's Scotbits were quoted as bid 88.1, offer 94.2 at the end of 1984. These values are quoted daily in the Press, and reflect the market value of the trust's investments. Units can be bought directly from the managers via advertisements in the Press, or through the bank or stockbroker. Unit trusts differ amongst themselves in their aims: some go

for high income, some for long-term growth, some invest in specific industries and some in a particular country. The frequent advertisements
usually define the aims of the trust.

The daily prices rise and fall just as do those of shares, and by and large
the performance of a trust is a measurement of the investment expertise of
its managers. This expertise can be judged by two magazines that compile
unit trust statistics, *Planned Savings* and *Money Management*. The performance of unit trusts in general during the last year (1984) was disappointing
to say the least. Only 13% of 597 unit trusts monitored outperformed the
All Share Index, although 64% did so in 1983. The best trust in 1984
(ManuLife High Income) made a gain of 54.2% over the year, while the
worst performer lost 21.2% of its value at the start of the year. Unit trust
managers like to feel that the investor buys and holds, and does not switch
in and out at frequent intervals. There is a school of thought, however, that
suggests that one year's winner will not repeat the performance the following year, and that one year's loser may turn out to be next year's winner.
This is a generalization that should be treated with caution—for example
the worst performer in 1983 only moved one place up the league table in
1984! However, it must be said that the principles that are put forward in
this book for maximizing your stock market performance apply equally well
to unit trusts, with allowance made for the fact that unit trust prices are not
as volatile as the shares that we will be interested in. Because of this lack
of volatility, the potential profits will not be as large, but of course, as there
is a spread of investments within a unit trust, the amount of risk involved
will be proportionally less.

A comparison of these various forms of investment is exceedingly complex when it is realized that interest rates and dividends are constantly fluctuating. If these factors are ignored, a meaningful comparison can be made
in terms of the capital sum committed to the original investment versus the
time which has elapsed since the investment was made. Quite obviously the
buying power of the pound has declined because of inflation over the middle part of this century. Because of this a 1900 pound is worth only 5p
today. Some monthly values of the Retail Price Index, taking Jan. 1974 as
100, are shown in Table 2.1. Investors should always be aware of this Index,
published monthly, since besides allowing him to adjust any gains he has
made for the effect of inflation, thereby injecting more realism into
achievements, it is a necessary part of the calculation of capital gains which
may accrue upon disposal of assets.

If the stock market is considered a reasonable place for investment, it
needs to protect the buying power of each pound invested by means of
growth in the market value of the securities held. Over a short term this may
not happen, whereas looking at the stock market over a longer term it has
been able to achieve this, as illustrated by the graph shown in Fig. 2.1. This

Table 2.1. Some monthly values of the Retail Price Index since 1982

	1982	1983	1984
Jan.		325.9	342.6
Feb.		327.3	344.0
Mar.	313.4	327.9	345.1
Apr.	319.7	327.3	349.7
May	322.0	333.9	
June	322.9	334.7	
July	323.0	336.5	
Aug.	323.1	338.0	
Sept.	322.9	339.5	
Oct.	324.5	340.7	
Nov.	326.1	341.9	
Dec.	325.5	342.8	

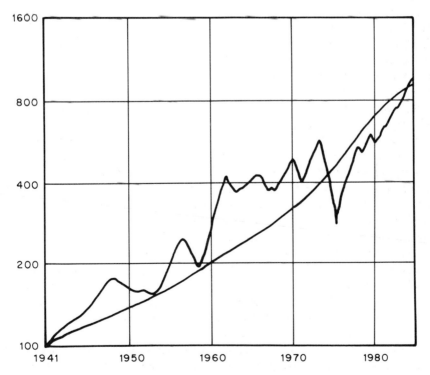

Figure 2.1. Share prices and the cost of living since 1941. The smooth line represents the cost of living while the more widely fluctuating line is the share price index. Both are given a value of 100 in 1941, and are plotted on a logarithmic scale. The time-scale is linear.

shows the cost of living and an index of share prices since 1941 to the end of 1984. Quite clearly it can be seen from the graph that share prices have more or less kept pace with the cost of living since 1941, judged by the fact that at the end of 1984 they were at approximately the same position on the vertical axis of the graph. This is of course over a time-scale of more than 40 years. We can, with some justification say that over the long term the market has consistently been a good hedge against inflation, even though during the middle 1970s it went through a patch in which it was less useful.

Figure 2.1 can be used to illustrate another point about the stock market. Quite obviously it can be seen that the growth in the stock market has not proceeded at a steady, uninterrupted rate, but has seen a number of short-term fluctuations, some of these of drastic proportions. If you were holding shares at the time, some of the short term falls were frightening in their suddenness and magnitude, while conversely there were rises that made investors euphoric for months on end. As an example, at the end of 1974 the index nose-dived to about a third of its mid-1972 value but then recovered strongly, and reached a then all-time high in 1979. An investor who, either through good luck or judgement, is able to take advantage of these short-term variations, can achieve a dramatic increase in the value of his holding compared with an investor who just buys and holds on. Taking an average share as an example, a person who sold his shares towards the end of 1972 could have used the proceeds to buy aboutt three times as many at the end of 1974.

Since the stock market offers us the chance, if we are fortunate, of making gains much higher than the 10% or so returns we expect from the other forms of investment discussed here, it is interesting to see the rapid way in which capital can be built up following a number of years of consistent good fortune. Table 2.2 shows the value of £100 investment at different rates of gain from 10% to 50% per annum, over various periods of time up to 30 years. While nobody is suggesting that we can consistently make 50% gains, year after year for 30 years, making us a millionaire 19 times over, we may well make 50% for a couple of years during the foreseeable future, and perhaps 20−30% for most of the others. If we could do this, then we would find our results moving somewhere towards the bottom right-hand corner of Table 2.1. However, we must not forget the shadow of the taxman hanging over us, and at the present time his interest starts as soon as we make over £5600 capital gains in a tax year.

Since investment in equities on the stock market is not a zero-risk process, an investor should not put at risk, at least while he is learning about the market, money he cannot afford to lose. He must also not put himself in the position of having to sell securities at what may be an unfavourable time in the normal market fluctuations in order to raise cash to repair his car or for some other such emergency. A policy of investment in the stock market

Table 2.2. Value of £100 invested at different rates of gain over various periods

Number of years	Rate of gain (or interest)				
	10%	20%	30%	40%	50%
1	110	120	130	140	150
2	121	144	169	196	225
3	133	173	220	274	338
4	146	207	286	384	506
5	161	249	371	538	759
6	177	299	483	753	1 139
7	195	358	627	1 054	1 709
8	214	430	816	1 476	2 563
9	236	516	1 060	2 066	3 844
10	259	619	1 379	2 893	5 767
20	673	3 834	19 005	83 668	332 526
30	1 745	23 738	262 000	2 420 143	19 175 106

must go along with the maintenance of a reasonable level of savings in a highly liquid form—in a bank or building society account, for example. When this state of affairs is achieved, the only reason for selling a particular holding will be that all the signals are saying that it has reached its highest point for the time being, and is expected to fall considerably in value in the immediate future.

Chapter 3

Is the Stock Market a Gamble?

Many people hold the view that stock market investment is just another form of gambling, just like betting on horses, dogs or cards. However, it is fairly easy to emphasize the distinction between gambling and informed investment. We can define gambling quite easily as the staking of money on situations in which the outcome is purely the workings of the laws of chance, or in some cases in which even the laws of chance have been manipulated against you. Fruit machines in which the percentage payout can be adjusted by the establishment are a case in point. It is instructive to consider the workings of chance. Thus, for example, the chance of a six coming up on on the throw of a die is exactly 1 in 6, because there are only six numbers on the die. Even if a six has not appeared for 50 throws, the chance for the next throw producing a six has not increased, it is still 1 in 6. The statisticians use the word probability instead of chance, and an important aspect is that probabilities have to be multiplied together. Thus the probability of throwing two sixes with two dice are 1/6 multiplied by 1/6, i.e. 1 chance in 36. Now, in the case of the purchase of shares, the question is, do share prices move according to the laws of chance? Are these movements totally random? If the answer to these questions is 'yes', then we might as well bet on the football pools or horses as put our hard-earned money into shares. Fortunately for us, the answer to these questions is not 'yes'; but neither is it 'no'. The best answer is that the movement of shares is *partially* random. After all, shares are bought and sold by *people*, and by and large, people do not act in a random manner. If they are investors they nearly all read the City pages of their newspaper, so that they take note of comment, they take note of the actual movement of share prices, and they all feel they know which section of the economy is doing well at a particular moment in time. Price movements are partially random in the sense that, given a certain share price today, we cannot tell whether the price will

14

be higher or lower in a year's time. What we can do, however, is say that, based on a knowledge of the behaviour of share prices over the recent past, we can find some point in time—not necessarily today— when the price of a particular share has a very high probability of moving higher over the following few weeks or months. By saying that share prices are partially random, we mean that their movement can be split into two parts: a random part and an ordered part. The ordered part is that caused by those investors who act more or less in unison, i.e. they all, at some point, consider that the market is moving in a direction, and they all happen to agree that the direction is up or the direction is down. The random part is caused by other investors who differ in their thinking about the direction of the market. Of course, these two groups are not well defined, and there is a constant exchange between them, i.e. an investor may follow the crowd for some of the time, and take a contrary view the rest of the time. Thus the amount of randomness in the market direction fluctuates with time, and, when we come to discuss the idea of trends in the stock market, we will begin to understand that the middle of a trend is that part of price movement which has the least random content, while the start and end of a trend is when the random content is highest.

A glance at any chart of a share price, or even the chart of the market as a whole in the form of the plot of the Financial Times Index, shows that share prices moves in waves. The random aspect of this motion is that the distance between waves, i.e. from peak to peak or trough to trough, is extremely variable, as also is the height of the waves, which may vary from a small ripple to the equivalent of a tidal wave. In addition, there is the aspect that we can have several waves superimposed upon each other, with one wave on the way down, and another, larger or smaller wave, going in the opposite direction.

Part of the reason for the existence of these ripples and waves is to be found in psychology. When a share price starts to move upwards, perhaps initially due to the laws of chance that at a particular time there are slightly more buyers than sellers of that share in the market, then other people begin to notice and also decide to buy. The process gathers momentum, causing an increasing share price, until such time as some of the holders of that share start to think that it cannot go on rising much longer, and decide to sell. More investors become aware that the price rise is slowing down, and these in turn become sellers, so causing the share price to fall. The height of the ripples or waves will depend upon the pressure of the demand of buyers over sellers, which is random, or at least partially random. The duration of the wave is random because we do not know for how long buyers will outnumber sellers; some random political or economic event, which is wholly unpredictable, may well cause the reversal of a particular trend, or there may even be no obvious reason for the change in sentiment.

The contrast between a totally random movement and the partially random movement which is the real picture for share prices can be illustrated
by Fig. 3.1. In Fig. 3.1(a) is shown the movement, over a 1-year period from
the beginning of April 1978 to the end of March 1979, of the shares of
Energy Services and Electronics Ltd. This was chosen because at that time
it was a popular share amongst small investors, and is becoming so once
more. During the period the share price did not move by more than 3.5p
over the course of any particular week. A computer program was set up to
generate completely random price movements, of any amount from 0 to
3.5p in 0.25p steps, either up or down. The result of plotting these computed price movements is shown in Fig. 3.1(b).

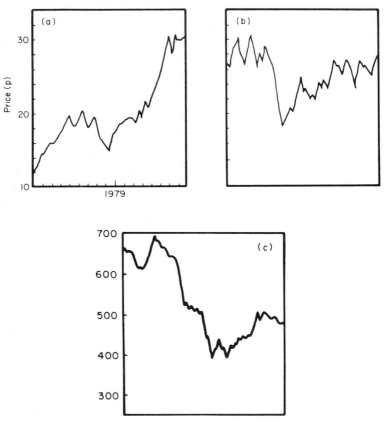

Figure 3.1. (a) The price movement of the shares of Energy Services and
Electronics Ltd between April 1978 and March 1979. (b) Totally random
movements of a mythical share price produced by a computer program: 52
points are plotted to simulate a year's prices. (c) The price movement of the
shares of Thorn—EMI Ltd during the year 1984.

At first glance (a) and (b) might appear to be very similar, implying that the shares of Energy Services and Electronics behaved over the period of time like the random movements produced by the computer. However, a closer inspection brings out two major ways in which these two graphs differ. Firstly, the number of price reversals, i.e. a change in direction from up to down or vice-versa, is much greater for the random case (these number 28) than for the real-life case where these number 16. This can be interpreted in terms of most of our investors thinking and acting in unison most of the time in the sense that they have decided which direction the price is headed and make the judgement that it will stay the same next week. The price reversals are caused by those investors who are taking an opposite view sometimes outnumbering the first category. The second major way in which the two graphs differ is that the random chart appears to be heading nowhere, in the sense that the price is oscillating about an (invisible) horizontal line. This would have been more obvious if we had plotted hundreds of such random points, and the reason for this journey to nowhere is that there is an equal probability of the price moving upwards or downwards in a random situation. This is the same as when we spin a coin. We may get five heads and one tail in the first six spins. If we took 1000 spins, then, provided the coin is evenly balanced, we would get close to 500 heads and 500 tails. A gambler backing heads would be unlikely to be far ahead at the end of a session of 1000 spins. So it is with shares if they were to behave randomly: an investor would be highly unlikely either to gain or to lose over a long period of time, but would come out roughly even. Now, if we look at the real situation of Energy Services, we find that the price was oscillating not about a horizontal line but about an upward-sloping line, not shown in the figure (such lines in the form of moving averages are shown in other examples throughout this book), but easily envisaged. An investor who bought at any time during the first half of the year could not have failed to sell at a profit in the latter half of the year. This is not to imply that all shares do this, even when the market in general is rising. Thus an investor buying Thorn–EMI in the first half of 1984 could not have avoided losing if he had sold during the second half of the year, as can be seen in Fig. 3.1(c). Again, the point made about the number of reversals and an overall direction of the share price (downwards!) in a real case as opposed to a random prediction is borne out. The aspect of the overall direction of a share price is covered more fully in Chapter 11, where it is shown how to analyse share prices for their underlying trends.

So, having agreed that share prices are partially random in their movement, and having pointed out in the last chapter that share prices on the whole are showing a long-term upward trend, we may ask ourselves if it is not sufficient to buy any share we fancy just when we feel like it, or when we have some unexpected money to spend. The answer is no, for two reasons. Firstly, it is only the market as a complete entity that is on an upward trend at the moment, and this does not mean that every share quoted on the Stock Exchange is doing the same thing. It is true that the market movement is the result of the vast majority of shares moving in that particular direction, but there is still a real chance that the very shares that you have bought are going to be the exceptions to the rule and will go down in value over a long period of time. A second point to be made is that the upward trend we are discussing is a *long-term* trend, so that if we do not envisage needing our money for 20 years or so, then we can probably get away with a policy of buying and forgetting.

The necessity for having a more logical approach than just buying and selling haphazardly can be illustrated readily by reference to actual share prices over two different 5-year periods. For simplicity we can take the high and low prices for the 30 constituent companies of the Financial Times Index for the years 1974 and 1978. Because of many changes in the constituents of the FT 30 Index between 1980 and 1984, only 24 companies remained in the Index for the latter period, but even so these data can still be used. Table 3.1 shows the high and low prices for 1974 and 1978 plus the average values of the share prices for each of the 2 years for the FT 30 constituents. Table 3.2 shows similar data for the years 1980 and 1984 for 24 of the FT 30 constituents. Note again that because of changes in the constituent companies, some companies shown in Table 3.1 are missing from Table 3.2, and have been replaced by others; for example J. Brown, Turner and Newall.

The reason for taking two quite separate periods is that the stock market has behaved rather differently in these two phases. The first period, 1974 to 1978, covered the stock market crash of late 1974, while the period 1980 to 1984 has shown a rather steadier upward pattern without such wild gyrations. Although the numerical results we will obtain from these two periods will be different, the principles which we can derive from them will be perfectly valid for either.

By using the figures in these tables we can define three types of investor, depending upon which price he paid for the shares, and which price he obtained when he sold them.

1. Mr Lucky. In 1974 Mr Lucky decided to buy shares in each of the 30 companies. Through good luck he just happened to choose the time when each of the shares was at its low value for the year. In 1978 Mr Lucky thought it was about time that he took his profit in order to shift his investment to some other enterprise. He fortunately chose a time to sell just as share prices were at their peak. Table 3.1 shows that Mr Lucky made an overall gain of 320.8% from the 30 shares during the period.

Table 3.1. Gains or losses from buying shares in the FT 30 constituent companies in 1974 and selling in 1978

	Buy at 1974 high, sell at 1978 low			Buy at 1974 low, sell at 1978 high			Buy at 1974 middle, sell at 1978 middle		
	Buy	Sell	Gain (loss)	Buy	Sell	Gain (loss)	Buy	Sell	Gain (loss)
Allied Brew.	79	78	(1.3)	30½	93½	206.6	54.8	85.8	56.6
Beecham	273	578	111.7	104	748	619.2	188.5	663.3	251.9
Blue Circle	236	150	(36.4)	118	296	150.8	177	223	26.0
BOC	49½	63½	28.3	14½	78½	441.4	32	71	121.9
Boots	109	184	68.8	46	237	415.2	77.5	210.5	171.6
Bowater	169½	163	(3.8)	69½	213	206.5	119.5	188	57.3
BP	590	720	22.0	190	954	402.1	390	837	114.6
J. Brown	131	217	65.6	41	481	1073.2	86	349	305.8
Cadbury Schweppes	59	48	(18.6)	20	61½	207.5	39.5	54.8	38.7
Courtaulds	112½	108	(4.0)	49	130	165.3	80.8	119	47.3
Distillers	152	163	7.2	62½	215	244.0	107.3	189	76.1
Dunlop	60	63	5.0	20	90	350.0	40	76.5	91.3
EMI	135	128	(5.2)	57	190	233.3	96	159	65.6
GEC	138	235	70.3	45	344	664.4	91.5	289.5	216.4
Glaxo	420	480	14.3	184	648	252.2	302	564	86.8
Grand Metropolitan	85	87	2.4	24	121½	406.3	54.5	104.3	91.4
GKN	220	248	12.7	93	296	218.3	156.5	272	73.8
Hawker Siddeley	306	315	2.9	122	630	416.4	214	472.5	120.8
ICI	247	328	32.8	115	421	266.1	181	374.5	106.9
Imperial Group	78½	71½	(8.9)	32	89	178.1	55.3	80.3	45.2
London Brick	51	61	19.6	16	80	400.0	33.5	70.5	110.4
Lucas	115	240	108.7	41	336	719.5	78	288	269.2
M & S	227	67½	(70.3)	95	94	(1.1)	161	80.8	(49.8)
P & O	138½	76	(45.1)	56½	118½	109.7	97.5	97.3	(0.2)
Plessey	101	87	(13.9)	36	125	247.2	68.5	106	54.7
Tate & Lyle	163	164	0.6	95	218	129.5	129	191	48.1
Tube Investments	291	336	15.5	120	436	263.3	205.5	386	87.8
Turner & Newall	125	156	24.8	61	209	242.6	93	182.5	96.2
UDS	97½	82	(15.9)	41	111	170.7	69.3	96.5	39.2
Vickers	121	160	32.2	65	211	224.6	93	185.5	99.5
Average gain			14.1%			320.8%			97.4%

Table 3.2. Gains or losses from buying shares in the FT30 constituent companies in 1980 and selling in 1984

	Buy at 1980 high, sell at 1984 low			Buy at 1980 low, sell at 1984 high			Buy at 1980 middle, sell at 1984 middle		
	Buy	Sell	Gain (Loss)	Buy	Sell	Gain (Loss)	Buy	Sell	Gain (Loss)
Allied Lyons	88.5	138	55.93	65.5	178	171.76	77	158	105.19
Beecham	174	285	63.79	109	390	257.80	141.5	337.5	138.52
Blue Circle	388	355	(8.51)	240	497	107.08	314	426	35.67
BOC	100	220	120.00	55.5	307	453.15	77.75	263.5	238.91
Boots	128	140	9.38	78.5	214	172.61	103.25	177	71.43
BP	502	395	(21.31)	320	540	68.75	411	467.5	13.75
Cadbury Schweppes	75.5	115	52.32	54.5	160	193.58	65	137.5	111.54
Courtaulds	87	108	24.14	50	160	220.00	68.5	134	95.62
Distillers	234	244	4.27	184	319	73.37	209	281.5	34.69
GEC	123	160	30.08	65	238	266.15	94	199	111.70
Glaxo	135	700	418.52	91	1100	1108.79	113	900	696.46
Grand Metropolitan	167	270	61.68	120	360	200.00	143.5	315	119.51
GKN	278	153	(44.96)	132	218	65.15	205	185.5	(9.51)
Hawker Siddeley	270	352	30.37	156	484	210.26	213	418	96.24
ICI	398	526	32.16	318	746	134.59	358	636	77.65
Imperial Group	89	134	50.56	69.5	180	158.99	79.25	157	98.11
Lucas	264	158	(40.15)	166	284	71.08	215	221	2.79
M & S	60.5	99	63.64	38	135	255.26	49.25	117	137.56
P & O	137	240	75.18	105	328	212.38	121	284	134.71
Plessey	94	188	100.00	35	248	608.57	64.5	218	237.98
Tate & Lyle	178	308	73.03	118	450	281.36	148	379	156.08
Thorn–EMI	378	375	(.79)	262	643	145.42	320	509	59.06
TI Group	312	164	(47.44)	188	290	54.26	250	227	(9.20)
Vickers	155	126	(18.71)	100	218	118.00	127.5	172	34.90
Average gain			45.13%			233.68%			116.22%

Having done so well in his previous dealings in the market, Mr Lucky thought he would have another go at the market in 1980. Since luck follows him everywhere, once again he was able to buy the 24 shares at a time when each of them was at its low for 1980. By 1984 Mr Lucky again turned his thoughts to other enterprises, and sold the 24 shares, fortunately once again finding the peak price for each share. Table 3.2 shows that Mr Lucky made a gain this time of 233.7% during the period.

2. Mr Unlucky. In 1974 Mr Unlucky decided to buy shares in all 30 companies of the FT30 Index. However, Mr Unlucky has never got anything right in his life. He thought that share prices in 1974, already at their peaks, were bound to continue upwards, so he bought at what turned out to be the highest prices reached in 1974. Four years later Mr Unlucky thought that share prices, already on their way down, were going to fall even further, and so he sold out at what turned out to be the lowest prices in 1978 for the 30 shares. From Table 3.1 it can be seen that Mr Unlucky made an overall gain of 14.1%. By 1980 Mr Unlucky had forgotten all about his bad experience in his previous outing in the market, and decided to buy the 24 shares of the FT30 Index again. Once again he bought at what turned out to be the high points of all his shares in 1980. By 1984 Mr Unlucky thought that the fall-back in prices was the start of a stock market crash, and decided to sell his holdings. He was unlucky enough to have sold out at the bottom of each of his FT30 shares. From Table 3.2 it can be seen that he made a gain of 45.1% in his shares over the 5-year period.

3. Mr Average. Mr Average also decided to buy shares in 1974, and took this decision just as the shares were at their mid-points for the year. By 1978 he decided to sell these shares and take his profit. He got out just as the shares were at their mid-points for 1978, gaining a profit of 97.4%. By 1980 Mr Average thought it was a good time to buy again, since shares were at a higher level than they had been earlier in the year. Once again he ended up buying the 24 of the FT30 shares at their mid-points for the year. In 1984 he again decided to sell, since he had made a reasonable profit on his investment, and sold at the middle of the price range for each of the 24 of the FT30 constituents. This time he achieved a gain of 116.2% over the period.

Of these three different types of investor, one was unfortunate enough to make gains of only 14.1% and 45.1% over the two periods, and might have been better off putting his money into a building society; one was lucky enough to make gains of 320.8% and 233.6% over each period; the third, average investor more or less doubled his money on each of the two occasions.

Now, of course, most of us would fall into the category of Mr Average rather than have Mr Lucky's good luck or Mr Unlucky's bad luck, because share prices tend to spend less time at the extreme high or low positions. We are more likely to buy, on a random basis, when prices are somewhere in between. The above examples show quite clearly the advantage of correct timing, both for buying and for selling, since bad timing (Mr Unlucky) gave returns of 14.1% and 45.1%, while perfect timing (Mr Lucky) gave returns of 320.8% and 233.6%. Thus the results when the timing was perfect were over 22 times better between 1974 and 1978 and over 5 times better between 1980 and 1984 than when the timing was totally wrong. The difference in these two factors (22 and 5) for the two periods is explained by the greater switchback nature of the market in the earlier period. In cases like this, where the yearly volatility of share prices is high, the advantage of correct timing becomes extremely marked.

Besides getting the timing of buying and selling operations correct, an equally important aspect of investment in the stock market is to make a correct *selection* of shares. Again, we can use Tables 3.1 and 3.2 to illustrate the point. This time we shall allow our three investors to choose five shares from the FT 30 constituents.

1. Mr Lucky. This man was lucky enough to purchase the very five shares which performed best over both the periods in question. For the period 1974 to 1978 he chose Beecham (619.2% gain), BOC (441.4% gain), John Brown (1073.2% gain), GEC (664.4% gain) and Lucas (719.5% gain). The average gain of these five shares was therefore a staggering 703.5% over the period. During his next venture into the market Mr Lucky chose BOC (453.1% gain), GED (266.1% gain), Glaxo (1108.7% gain), Plessey (608.5% gain) and Tate & Lyle (281.3% gain). The average gain of these five shares over the period was 343.5%.

2. Mr Unlucky. This poor man unwittingly chose the five worst performers over the period. He selected Blue Circle (loss of 36.4%), Cadbury Schweppes (loss of 18.6%), Marks & Spencer (loss of 70.3%), P & O (loss of 45.1%) and UDS (loss of 15.9%). The loss over this period was 37.3%. Thinking this was just one bad experience that could not possibly be repeated, Mr Unlucky entered the market again in 1980. This time he bought BP (loss of 21.3%), GKN (loss of 44.9%), Lucas (loss of 40.1%), TI Group (loss of 47.4%) and Vickers (loss of 18.7%). The average loss over this period was therefore 34.4%.

3. Mr Average. Mr Average chose shares which were the middle five out of the gains/losses column for buying and selling at middle prices in 1974 and 1978. He bought Distillers (76.1% gain), Dunlop (91.3% gain), Glaxo (86.8% gain), Grand Metropolitan (91.3% gain) and

Tube Investments (87.8% gain). This resulted in an overall gain of 86.7%. In 1980 Mr Average again bought shares which were in the middle of the gains/losses column for the 24 shares shown in Table 3.2. This time he bought Allied Lyons (105.1% gain), Boots (71.6% gain), Courtaulds (95.6% gain), Hawker (96.2% gain) and ICI (77.6% gain). This resulted in an overall gain of 108.8%.

These results show how important it is not only to achieve the best timing possible for the buying and selling operations, but to select the correct shares to buy in the first place. The correct choice improved Mr. Lucky's gain from 320.8% to 703.5% on his 1974 buying operation, and improved the gain from 233.7% to 343.5% during 1980–84. On the other hand, a bad choice of shares for Mr Unlucky turned his small gain of 14.1% into a large loss of 37.3% for the 1974 operation. For his 1980 foray into the market the gain of 45.1% was turned into a loss of 34.4%. In the case of Mr Average, we would not expect the gains from five shares chosen as being in the middle of the group of 30 and 24 shares respectively in terms of performance to be very much different from the behaviour of the group as a whole, since of course, mathematically speaking, the average of each group will end up somewhere in the middle of the price range. This turns out to be the case in practice, since the gains from selecting the five middle shares were 86.7% and 108.8%, compared with 97.4% and 116.2% for the groups as a whole.

No doubt, at this point, most of us would probably say that we would be quite happy to be in Mr Average's position, with gains of between 86.7% and 116.2%. The point is, though, that Mr Average did not make his gains through exercising his intelligence, but merely through having the good luck to avoid taking the disastrous decisions of Mr Unlucky. There is no guarantee that luck would run the same way for us, and we may indeed turn out to be about as unsuccessful as Mr Unlucky. As serious investors, a policy based simply on luck should have no part to play in our investment philosophy. So we have to develop methods which are based upon logical timing and selection procedures which themselves are made as objective as possible.

As far as timing is concerned, there are of course two areas in which we have to exercise judgement: knowing when to buy and when to sell. It is interesting that the tipsters in most newspapers have a blind spot when it comes to selling shares which they have tipped strongly as buying situations some time earlier. You are most unlikely, however closely you study the financial pages of your newspaper, to find a recommendation to sell a particular share, whether it is a share which that columnist implored you to buy at the beginning of the year, or another one which he did not mention as a buy, but which is known to be popular among small investors. A moments's thought will tell you that buying and selling are equally critical operations and correct buying procedures can be ruined by a failure to sell at the right time. It is no use telling your friends how clever you were to buy XYZ at 120p when they reached 200p if you are still left holding them when they have plunged to 90p. Certainly you were clever to have bought at 120, but you would have been cleverer still if you had sold at 190 when XYZ started to fall back from their peak.

The two areas of buying and selling require different approaches, and so in this book separate chapters are devoted to when to buy and when to sell. It is amply demonstrated that it is possible to develop methods which consistently give us a buying signal at the low end of the price range of a share and consistently gives us a selling signal at the top end of the range. It is certain therefore that we can, by using these methods, improve upon the performance of an investor who just picks his buying time, selling time, and the share in question, more often than not at random.

It should be stressed, and a study of the methods outlined in the two chapters on buying and selling will underline this, that it is not possible *at the time* to determine that a share is at its low or high value. The end of an upward or downward trend in the market for a particular share is a random event. We have already mentioned the *partially random* nature of share price movements, and pointed out the existence of trends as evidence

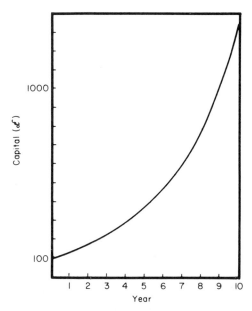

Figure 3.2. The growth in capital over a 10-year period when a consistent gain of 30% is made each year.

for the partially predictable nature of share prices. Once the trend has been under way for some time it becomes more and more probable that it is going to end. It is the exact time of the ending of the trend that is unknown until after it has occurred and a new trend in the opposite direction, or even sideways, is in being. The best timing methods will tell us as soon as possible — in terms of days or a few weeks at most— that the direction of movement has changed. By knowing as soon as possible that the direction has changed, we will be able to buy at prices not very far upwards from the actual low, and sell at prices not far down from the high value.

The selection procedure which we put forward in this book is based upon two premises. Firstly that shares which vary the most between their high and low values, and have done so for a number of years, will continue to do the same in the future, at least in the near future. A second consideration is that some shares are obviously not falling as much as the rest of the market dur-

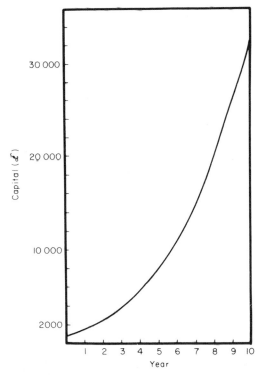

Figure 3.3. The growth in capital over a 10-year period when a consistent gain of 30% is made and additional sums are added. In this case the starting amount is £1000 and £500 is added each year.

ing a general decline. These shares can be considered to be amongst the strongest in the market, and therefore should advance the most when the market recovers. Once again it is amply demonstrated that this selection procedure is a vast improvement upon a random selection based just upon personal feeling or newspaper tips.

An investor who follows the rules for selection and timing of purchases and sales outlined in the following chapters should hope to see a return on his investment considerably higher than the rate of inflation.

The rapid rise in capital which occurs when compounding such a gain each year is shown in Fig. 3.2. An investor starting with £100 will be worth £1379 after 10 years, while starting with £1000 should see him £13 790 to the good after 10 years.

Probably most investors would be adding an amount each year to their original investment. In this case the capital appreciates at a tremendous rate. As an example we could take an investor who starts with £1000 and adds to this a sum of £500 each year. His holdings would follow the curve shown in Fig. 3.3 if he makes a gain of 30% each year. At the end of 10 years his £30 000-plus should enable him to look life's little financial disasters in the eye! Of course, these figures assume the lucky investor is living in tax exile, and it should be pointed out that there is a capital gains tax liability once (at the time of writing) the gains exceed £5600 during the tax year.

Chapter 4

Buying, Selling and Reading the News

To most people the Stock Exchange is something of a mystery. It is a place where fortunes are made overnight, whose members live in large houses somewhere in Surrey and travel to the City in a first-class compartment. While some of this is true, it is not generally realized how many people are directly and indirectly involved in the workings of the Stock Exchange. Since the British Telecom launch it has been estimated that some 3 million individuals own shares directly; for example, ICI has about ½ million shareholders, while British Telecom has nearly 2 million. The rest of the population are indirectly involved in security ownership through large institutions, such as life insurance offices, pension funds, trade unions, building societies, banks, etc. These have huge resources to invest—tens of millions of pounds each week for life insurance offices alone—and a large proportion of these funds are used to buy stocks and shares. There can hardly be a person in the UK who has no life insurance, does not belong to a pension fund, does not belong to a trade union, and does not deposit money in a bank or building society, however temporarily. Even if such a person exists, he is a resident of a country whose government raises money through the Stock Exchange, and the company he works for may well do the same.

How the idea of a Stock Exchange began is not known, but it was tied up with the increase in trade from Elizabethan times onwards. All sorts of enterprises grew up in which numbers of people wished to participate. Since new participants may have wished to pull out of an enterprise or even invest more money in it, a market-place grew up in which buyers and sellers could meet, usually through an agent. As governments also wished to raise loans, usually in order to wage war, this function also became part of the working of the market.

From its original beginnings as a part of the market place in the Royal Exchange the stock market moved to its own premises in 1773, using the name 'Stock Exchange', and then to its present site at the beginning of the nineteenth century. Today the Stock Exchange occupies a 26-storey tower block.

The workings of the Stock Exchange are peculiar to London. In New York, where Wall Street has the largest exchange in the world, the buying and selling of stocks and shares is carried out by stockbrokers who deal with each other. In London, brokers have to use special dealers known as jobbers. The jobbers are stationed at pitches on the 'Floor' of the Stock Exchange, and are responsible for setting buying and selling prices. Only a few jobbers will deal with any one security. A jobber is only interested in a particular group of securities and will buy or sell these. Jobbers have to judge market trends, and their profit or loss depends on the difference between buying and selling prices, which can vary by the minute.

The broker's job is to carry out the wishes of his client, who may be a buyer or a seller of a particular security. He goes to each of the jobbers who deal in that security and ascertains the buying and selling prices quoted by each jobber. The latter, incidentally, does not know, when he quotes prices, whether the broker wishes to buy or sell that particular security. The broker then buys or sells, as necessary, the security with the jobber quoting the most attractive price. The broker will always obtain the best deal possible for his client, who may be you, the individual, or a bank acting on your instructions, or a big institutional investor. Both jobber and broker note the bargain in a little book, and the shares are then yours, if you are buying, or the proceeds yours if you are selling. However, as explained later, the paperwork for the transaction takes a while to catch up, but if you are a buyer you may still sell your shares, the same day if you wish, before you receive your share certificates.

The beginner, making his first few purchases and sales of shares, can carry out these operations by walking into his bank and then giving instructions in writing to buy or sell so many shares of X. Within a day or so he will receive a contract note setting out the transaction and the total sum to be paid (including stamp duty, commission, etc.) or the total being credited to his account. These moneys will not be due until settlement day, which is normally the Tuesday 11 days after the end of the fortnightly account. Thus shares purchased on the first day of the account will not have to be paid for for about 3 weeks. Eventually the share certificates will arrive at the bank and be retained by them, unless you specifically ask for them.

For the serious investor it is best to have your own broker, since besides the simple operation of buying and selling, the broker provides a number of services. He can tell you about the standing of the individual companies, the industrial sectors which are progressing the most rapidly, current economic trends and the like. You cannot just walk into a broker's office, however, and ask him to deal for you. You can either be introduced by someone who is a client of the broker, or you can write to the Secretary of the Stock Exchange, London EC2, and ask for a list of brokers. From this list, select a broker (the Stock Exchange will not recommend one) and write to him asking if he will take you as a client, giving the name and address of your bank as a reference. Once he is happy about your ability to pay for any securities you buy, you can either telephone or write your instructions to buy or sell as necessary.

The instructions to your broker should be as clear as possible, and normally, in the event of buying, you should quote a limit above which you are not prepared to buy; otherwise your broker may be buying the shares at the top of a daily price range, which would not have happened if you had set a limit which was lower than this. Your broker may well call you to say he cannot buy at the limit you have set, and quotes the best possible price he can obtain. You can either accept that and tell him to go ahead and buy at that price, or ask him to keep the limit on for a day or so. However, one has to be realistic, and if the market price of your shares is improving constantly, either buy at the best price your broker quotes you or look for some other share.

The cost of buying shares is somewhat higher than the cost of selling, because of government stamp duty on purchases. As a rough guide, the detailed costs of buying and selling 300 shares at a buying price of 136p and a selling price of 124p are given below:

Buying		Selling	
300 shares @ 136p,		300 shares @ 124p,	
consideration	£408.00	consideration	£372.00
add transfer stamp	9.00	*less* contract stamp	0.10
add contract stamp	0.10	*less* commission	7.00
add commission	7.00	*less* VAT on commission	1.05
add VAT on commission	1.05		
Total	£425.15	Total	£363.85

So, taking into account the actual cost of buying the shares, you have paid about 141.7p per share as opposed to the quoted price of 136p, and receive about 121p per share compared with the quoted price of 124p. Before you can make a profit on a 'round trip' of buying and then selling the same share, the price would have to rise from 136p, the buying price, to a selling price of about 145p, i.e. a gain of about 7%. If you hold the shares for a period which includes the payment of a dividend, the latter may well offset these buying and selling costs.

Transactions of the sort of amounts shown above attract the heaviest dealing expenses. The commission will become smaller as a percentage once the consideration exceeds certain amounts. Once the commission exceeds £5000 a levy called the CSI levy, being at present a charge of 60p, applies to the transaction.

At some point, preferably before you buy shares, but certainly after you own a piece of a company, you will be following the fortunes of your selected company in the financial press. You will also receive, from time to time, glossy brochures containing balance sheets etc., and with some companies a list of shareholders' perks which you may receive, such as a percentage knocked off the cost of a Channel crossing, dry cleaning for half-price, and so on. It is going to be essential for you to understand the entries in the share price pages of newspapers, and have some ability to extract the essential data from company reports.

READING THE FINANCIAL PRESS

The world of finance, as any other activity, generates its own jargon and shorthand which makes it difficult for the newcomer to understand what is being said. Appendix C is a glossary which lists just about all the expressions and words you are likely to come across. There is one area, however, which needs some expansion, and that is an explanation of the various columns of figures normally found in the share price pages of newspapers. A few typical entries are shown in Table 4.1.

The figures in the columns 1985 'High' and 'Low' are the highest and lowest prices achieved by the security during the year. At the end of the year, in order to achieve a carry-over, the column would be headed, for example, 1985/86, but the 1985 figures will be dropped usually around mid-April, at the end of the stock exchange account in which the last day of the income tax year falls. These figures are useful in telling us where today's price stands in relation to the highs and lows, i.e. is the share making a new high, or a new low, or has it risen some way from its low value?

Under the heading 'Share' we find the name of the company and the type

Table 4.1. Typical headings and figures on the share price pages of various newspapers

1985								
High	Low	Share	Price	Change	Div. (net)	Cover	Yield (gross)	P/E
288	206	Polly Pck Intl 10p	270	− 5	3.5	10.00	1.9	5.6
£124	£102	Polly Pck 9pc Cv Ln '03–08	£123	− 1	9.0		7.4	

and nominal value of the share. In this book we are only concerned with ordinary shares, which simply have a name such as Polly Peck Intl. 10p, which means the share has a nominal value of 10p when first issued. The nominal value, if not given, is taken to be 25p. For Polly Peck, however, we can see there are two entries, Polly Peck Intl 10p and Polly Peck 9% Cv Ln '03–08—short for 9% Convertible Loan, 2003–2008. The latter entry is for a loan stock. When this was issued, the nominal or par value of the stock was £100, although it might have been issued at a price slightly more or less than this. The interest was fixed at 9% per £100 of stock, so that the present holder gets £9 per annum for each £100 of stock irrespective of the price he may have had to pay for it, which varied between £102 and £124 in 1985. The 'Convertible' 03–08 label means that the holder has the option to convert the stock into ordinary shares, and that the maturity date is between 2003 and 2008.

The terms for conversion for the loan stocks of companies will differ from company to company. Loan stocks are more secure than ordinary shares in the sense that the interest will be paid, whereas dividends on ordinary shares may not, and if a company runs into difficulties the loan stock will be repaid first before ordinary shares. Between loan stocks and ordinary shares in terms of repayment if a company runs into trouble will be so-called 'Preference' share. Not many of these have voting rights in the company. Most ordinary shares carry voting rights in the company, but there is another type of ordinary share also, called the 'non-voting' share or 'A' shares. The practice of having a 'second-class shareholder' in terms of a say in the way a company is run is to be deplored, and this lack of a voice in company affairs is reflected in the quoted price of non-voting shares, which are invariably lower than their vote-carrying counterparts.

It follows from the above that ordinary shares are the risk capital, so that the holders do well in terms of dividends if the company is prospering, but do badly when things go wrong. Most companies do not pay out all their surplus profits in the form of dividends, but hold on to part of them.

Sometimes these accumulated surpluses are issued as 'free' shares, usually called 'scrip issue' or a 'capital issue'.

The column headed 'Prices' gives the closing price of that share the previous day. It usually represents a middle value between the buying and selling price, so that if you are buying, you will almost certainly have paid a little more, and if you are selling, will receive a little less than the listed price. The 'change' column is simply whether the price has moved up [+] or down [−], and the amount of movement since the previous day's close. An unchanged price may have a hyphen, row of dots or be left blank.

The 'Div. net' is the dividend actually paid per share. Usually dividends are paid twice-yearly, the first payment being called the interim and the second payment the final dividend.

The cover is the ratio of the profit the company made to the amount of money it paid out in dividends, so telling us how much of the company profits found their way to the shareholders.

The gross yield is derived from the dividend relative to the share price before applying advanced Corporation Tax at the rate pertaining at the time.

The P/E (price to earning) ratio is calculated by dividing the earnings per share into the share price. Thus supposing a company made £20.5 million, and its ordinary capital is £80 million, the shares have a par value of 25p. If the present share price is say 90p, then the P/E ratio is:

$$\frac{0.90 \times 80}{20.5 \times 0.25} = 14.0$$

SHOULD WE PAY MUCH ATTENTION TO FINANCIAL NEWS?

So far we have been dealing with facts as reported in the financial press, i.e. dividends and share prices. However, the other aspect of the financial Press, the airing of opinions and reasons for the behaviour of the market, has to be taken very cautiously. This can be illustrated very easily by quoting the reasons for a movement of the Financial Times Index, one barometer of the market, over a fairly short period of time, as given in the same newspaper.

1. Fears of an impending general election sent investors diving for cover. The Index fell 6.7, on sustained selling.
2. Confidence in the near certainty of a general election with a consequent Conservative victory caused what some brokers described as panic buying in the markets yesterday. The Index recorded a gain of 10.2.
3. The large rise in the value of the pound on foreign exchange markets has led to increasing nervousness about the ability of British industry to re-

main competitive in overseas markets. The gloom was reflected in stock markets by a fall of 8.2 in the FT Index.

4. The increasing value of the pound saw foreign investors piling into gilts yesterday. The confidence spilled over into the equity markets, which saw its largest 1-day rise, 8.5, for several months.

5. The prospect of a give-away budget fuelling a mini-consumer boom had investors out in force yesterday. The stores sector registered some solid gains and the index rose six points.

6. Uncertainty about the contents of the forthcoming budget resulted in a downward drift in the markets yesterday. The stores sector was particularly hard hit, with Marks & Spencer shedding 5p. The index ended the day 4.7 points down.

7. John Bull & Co announced profits up 30% on last year. The final dividend was increased 50% to 4.5p to give a total of 8.5p. The shares fell 3p to 115.

8. The Chairman's statement underlined the fact that 1985 will be a difficult trading year. The value of the pound causing difficulty in foreign markets allied to the deepening world recession makes it likely that a number of plants will have to go on short time. The shares gained 2p to 258p.

The above statements fall into two categories. In the first six the commentators are trying to square the behaviour of the market as a whole with the overall political or economic climate. It makes no sense that one day a strong pound can be considered to be a reason for selling shares, while a few days later a strong pound is a reason for buying shares. The reasons for the behaviour of the market are almost certainly more subtle than that.

In the next two statements the shares appear to behave in a contrary fashion to that which one would expect from the company news. The reason is that the news has already been either known for certain by those with the right contacts, or has been guessed at by the 'clever money'. Thus the good news or bad news has been already discounted in the share price.

The essential point which the foregoing is meant to convey is that an investor who buys or sells according to financial news is unlikely to be successful. An investor has to join the ranks of those people who are ahead of the news. How? Well, quite straightforwardly, in fact, if one makes the reasonable assumption that the activities of those investors who are ahead of the market will be reflected by a movement in the price of the shares concerned. It is by following the prices of shares that we can therefore make buying or selling decisions in good enough time to make a superior profit compared with those who wait until it is too late. The breaking of news, good or bad, is then more or less irrelevant to us, since we will have already taken action. In a great many cases we will not be surprised by such news, since we will be very well aware of the price movements caused by those who either have inside knowledge or have made educated guesses.

Chapter 5

When to Buy

The market in securities, as any other market, is a place of shifting values, depending upon supply and demand, which in turn reflect investor psychology. In order to come to any conclusions about the market we have to have some means of measuring it. The most widely quoted measurement of the market is the Financial Times Industrial Ordinary (FT30) Index. The Index is derived from the prices of 30 leading equities, covering all sectors of the market. These are listed in Table 5.1.

Readers of the first edition of this book will notice that this list in Table 5.1 has changed since 1980. This point was also made in Chapter 3. Every so often one of the shares used in the calculation of the Index will be replaced by another. One obvious time when this will happen is if one of the constituent companies is taken over by another.

Since the market is composed of thousands of shares, it may be asked whether the FT Index truly reflects the state of the market. In order to decide on this it is necessary to look at how the Index is calculated from the prices of its 30 constituents. The FT30 Index is a geometric mean of the

Table 5.1. Constituents of the Financial Times 30 Index.

Allied Lyons	Cadbury Schweppes	London Brick
Associated Dairies	Courtaulds	Lucas Industries
Beecham Group	Distillers	Marks & Spencer
BICC	GEC	P & O
Blue Circle	Glaxo Holdings	Plessey
BOC International	Grand Metropolitan	Tate & Lyle
Boots	GKN	Thorn EMI
Bowater Corp	Hawker Siddeley	TI Group
BP	ICI	Trusthouse Forte
BTR	Imperial Group	Vickers

prices of its components. Because of this, it has a built-in pull downwards, i.e. it tends to be rather pessimistic of market behaviour. This can be illustrated by imagining a similar index constructed from only two shares. Suppose the shares are both valued at 200p. The Index is then $\sqrt{(200 \times 200)} = 200$.

Now, if one share moves up to 300p and the other down to 100p, then an investor holding both of these would see no change in his total investment, since their average price would still be 200p. The new index, however, would be $\sqrt{(300 \times 100)} = 173.2$. Thus the Index has fallen although the value of the portfolio has remained unchanged. You can work out for yourself that, except if the two prices move exactly the same amount, this Index is always less than the usual arithmetic average, calculated by taking half of the sum of the two prices.

There are several other indices available, for example the FT Actuaries All Share Index and the Financial Times Stock Exchange 100 Index, FTSE-100. Like the FT30 Index, none of these tells the real truth. The FT30 Index has the advantage that it is widely quoted, appearing in all those newspapers that have a City section, is given in the financial news on radio and television and is available via the telephone recorded service. Because the FTSE-100 Index has only been available for just over a year, we would be unable to use it in this book to demonstrate market turning points over the longer time-scale needed to develop investment principles. In passing it may be noted that, just as in the case of the FT30 Index, the 100 constituents of the FTSE-100 Index have undergone several changes in its brief history. Because of its ready availability, we shall therefore use the FT30 Index in this book as a means of deciding on market turning points.

THE PAST: A HELP WITH THE FUTURE

The only evidence upon which we can base any prediction of the immediate or long-term future of the market is by a study of its past history. The past gives us an indication of how the market reacted to various factors and it is not too far-fetched to believe that a recurrence of the same factors will have an effect on the market. Of course, from time to time new factors occur which have not been encountered before, such as the impact of North Sea oil, but these can be treated on their merits. We are concerned with the trends that develop as a result of these various factors, especially with the fact that the trends last for appreciable time-periods, so that when their existence is determined there is still plenty of movement left in the same direction. Because of this it is then possible to take an investment position with a high degree of certainty of profit.

An important feature of the market is its volatility, which we may define as the rate at which it goes up or down. We can gain an impression of this from plotting the Financial Times Index over a period of time. If the Index rises or falls a substantial amount, say 20% or so, in a period of a few days, then obviously we would describe it as volatile, whereas if it took 5 years to rise or fall this amount, then we would say it was involatile. From our point of view, the degree of volatility is crucial to the determination of the time for which we remain invested, i.e. are we going to buy one week and sell the next, or are we talking in terms of periods of years between these two actions? The question of volatility is also important in deciding for how long we have to follow the market before we can decide if it is rising or falling. To illustrate this point, the daily plot of the Index for 1 week (10–14 December 1984) is shown in Fig. 5.1. Now, is it possible to decide from this whether the market is rising or falling? Well, the market does appear to be going up by virtue of the fact that it started the week at 930.3 and ended up at 935.4. Now, remembering that we have to have a gain of at least 5% in order to clear our buying and selling commissions, then, if we look at the Index as a share in which we can invest, clearly we would not have made a profit in buying on Monday at 930.3 and selling on Friday at 935.4, or even buying on the Wednesday when the index fell to 922.3 and then selling at 935.4. Figure 5.1 is fairly typical of the market, in the sense that it is extremely rare, say on no more than 3 or 4 weeks a year, for the market to rise or fall by 5% or more in a week. There are, of course, many

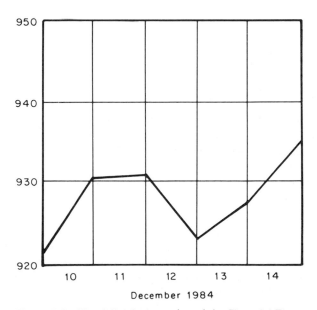

Figure 5.1. The daily closing value of the Financial Times Index from 10th to 14th December 1984.

individual shares that do much better or much worse than that, but at the moment we are only concerned with the whole market. So, Fig. 5.1 tells us one thing—our buying and selling must cover a larger period than a week if we are to make a profit since, with only a few exceptions which it would be difficult to predict in advance, the market is not volatile enough to deal on such a short time-scale.

Now, can we use Fig. 5.1 to tell us something else; namely if we are contemplating buying, is that particular week a good week to buy, since we have shown a week in which the Index has risen over the 5-day period? Conversely, if we had shown a Figure in which the Index has fallen to about the same extent over the week, would that have told us if it was the time to sell if we had been holding some shares? The answer is that next week's market may or may not continue in the same direction. For the short period we are discussing, the market finished the following week at 924.3 and the week after that at 945.2. Quite obviously, then, the behaviour of the market over 1 week tells us virtually nothing about the climate for investment. One may well ask at this point if we can ever decide which way the market is moving. The answer is yes, but only if we look at a large enough time-period, the time-period being sufficient to encompass much greater movements in the market. From past history there frequently occur periods in which swings of 20% in the FT Index occur within some 3 months or so. Thus, in order to decide on the current direction of the market, we should look at the last 3 months' weekly closing values of the Index at the very least, and preferably even a longer period.

For our purposes, since we are trying to establish as good a picture of the market as possible, we should look at a time-scale of the order of 10 years or so. Already in Chapter 2 we have shown how shares have performed compared with the cost of living since 1941 (Fig. 2.1). The disadvantage of Fig. 2.1 is that although it gives an indication that the market has zig-zagged up and down, and that the underlying trend is upwards, it does not show us the fine detail of the week-to-week variations. In order to do this, the movement of the FT Index since 1967 is shown in Fig. 5.2. The immediate impact of this figure is that the market has moved in waves, with troughs every 4 years or longer apart. Superimposed upon these large waves we have smaller ones, of a few months or so duration, and finally upon these we have ripples which are normally of a few weeks' duration. The larger waves, small waves and ripples may not always be moving in the same direction— we may have a small wave which is falling, taking prices down, but is superimposed on a large wave which is trending upwards. In such a case our shares may show a loss in the short term, but the price will eventually recover. On the other hand, the small wave may be causing an upward lift to prices when the underlying trend is downwards. To buy at such a time with a view to holding for a reasonable length of time may see the initial

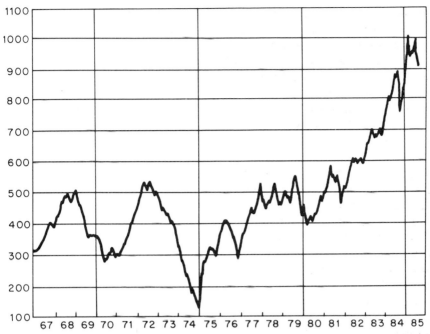

Figure 5.2. The movements of the Financial Times Index over the period since 1967. The vertical scale is linear.

profit quickly eroded. Quite obviously, timing of our investment buying is absolutely crucial, and in this chapter we are going to develop methods which will enable us to take advantage of large waves, small waves and even ripples of a few weeks' duration. We will see that it is possible to use a ripple profitably even when the underlying longer-term trend of the market is downwards.

These waves and ripples are the result of a struggle between two groups of people. In stock market parlance they are called 'bulls' and 'bears'. Bulls are optimists, who think that at this particular moment share values are set for an increase, and so they buy. Bears think the opposite, that the market is about to go down, and that the time has come to sell. Sometimes they feel so strongly about this that they sell shares they have not got, with a view to buying them back later at a lower price to pass back to the previous buyer via the broker. At any one time there will always be these two sorts of operators in the stock market, but they will rarely be in balance. When bulls predominate the market will go up, and when bears predominate the market will go down. The ratio of these two sets of people will vary according to their interpretation of various news items, both political and business, upon other investors, as well as their overall feeling about the economy in general and the stock market in particular.

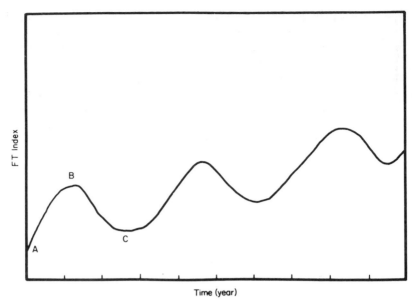

Figure 5.3. An idealized version of the movements of the Financial Times Index over a period of years.

If, for the moment, we ignore the short-term variations, an idealized version of the FT Index over a number of years would look like that in Fig. 5.3. From point A to B, a bull phase, more and more investors and investing institutions become filled with optimism about share prices, and put more and more money into the market, pushing up share prices and hence the Index. At point B the smart operators, and those of you who have taken note of the contents of this book, will realize that it cannot go on for ever and that it is time to get out. Gradually the amount of selling starts to outweigh the amount of buying and the market and Index starts on a downward journey. The degree of pessimism then also starts to increase. Many investors get their fingers burnt by failing to sell at, or soon after, point B, and watch their share values fall to point C. At this point many of them are so shattered by the experience that they sell out, and never invest in the market again. By the time point C is reached, many of the experienced investors realize that the fall has to end some time, and they piece together enough optimistic facts from the business news to convince themselves that it is time to start buying again. This starts a new upward trend, which develops its own momentum as more and more investors climb on the bandwagon to begin the heady climb again. The whole process repeats itself time and again over the years, while some investors get richer and some poorer.

These variations are nothing to be frightened about, and can be used to our advantage, since we can make larger profits from such gyrations in the market then from a situation in which the market is climbing slowly in a fairly straight line. This can be illustrated by putting some theoretical (but fairly typical) values to the Index, and pretending that the Index is a share in which we are investing where the values would imply the share price in pence. We can then compare the results obtained by an investor who buys at the beginning of the long term and sells at the end with those obtained by someone who buys and sells several times at the appropriate intermediate bottoms and tops.

Point	Corresponding FT Index
A	200
B	300
C	250
D	350
E	300
F	400
G	350

If we invest £200 at point A, we can then sell at point B for £300. At point C this £300 would then buy 300/2.50 = 120 shares. The 120 shares will rise in value and be worth $120 \times £3.50 = £420$ at point D. This £420 will buy 420/3.00 = 140 shares at point E. These 140 shares at point F are worth $140 \times £4.00 = £560$.

Therefore, starting with £200 at point A, by a series of buying and selling at the troughs and peaks, the investment becomes worth £560, i.e. a gain of 180%. Compared with this, an investor who buys at point A, investing £200, will be able to realize £400 at point F, i.e. he has a profit of 100%.

What may be a surprise to some investors is that a profit can still be made by buying and selling at the appropriate times even when the longer-term trend is downwards. Take the following values of the FT Index at points A to F as an example:

Point	Corresponding FT Index
A	350
B	400
C	300
D	350
E	250
F	300

Suppose in this case, to make the figures simpler, that we invest £350 at point A. The shares can be sold at point B for £400. This will buy 133 shares at point C, which rise in value to $133 \times £3.50 = £465.5$ at point D. This amount of money will buy 186 shares at point E where they are 250p each, and finally they can be sold for £558.6 at F. Therefore the initial investment has made a gain of 59.6%. Compared with this, an investor who bought at A and sold at F would have made a loss of 14.3%.

So, in both of these cases, the members of the buy-and-hold brigade would have come out way behind an investor who takes advantage of the intermediate ups and downs in share values. Of course, in these calculations, the cost of buying and selling shares has been neglected, but it is fair to take the view that the dividends yielded by an average portfolio more or less cover the costs of the various transactions, so that these costs can be considered to have a minimal effect on the profit and loss picture.

The situation we were discussing is rather an artificial one, mainly for two reasons. Firstly, it is never possible to buy consistently at an exact bottom and sell at an exact top, and anyone who claims to be able to do this can probably also walk on water. Secondly, we have been discussing not an actual share, but the market in general. The market in general is of course composed of thousands of shares, and while the market is rising, most, but not all, of these shares will do the same; although some will gain more than others. Conversely, when the market is falling, most shares will fall, although a few will manage to register gains during that time.

This can be illustrated by Fig. 5.4, in which is shown the plots of several hypothetical shares, and the plot of the overall market in these shares, as indicated by an average of the prices of all these shares. In what we might call the topping region, which is a few weeks or even months either side of the actual top of the average of all these shares, we have shown one share topping out in advance of the market, one share topping out at the same time as the market, one share topping out later than the market, and finally a 'rogue' share which is going its own way. Next there is a bottoming region, which again is a few weeks or months either side of the market bottom. Once more, we have a share that bottoms in advance of the market, one share bottoming at the same time, one share reaching its lowest point later than the market, and in addition, our rogue share has been steadily rising while the rest of the market has been falling. It should be pointed out here that a share which tops out ahead of the market does not necessarily bottom ahead of the market, and the same is true of a share which tops out later than the market. As far as we are concerned, whether a share tops out early or late after we have bought it is irrelevant, for each share will be giving its signal to us when it has reached its peak.

The most important aspect in this discussion is that in the region which we have labelled the bottoming region, most shares are either just about to reach their lowest values, or have just risen from their lowest values. The

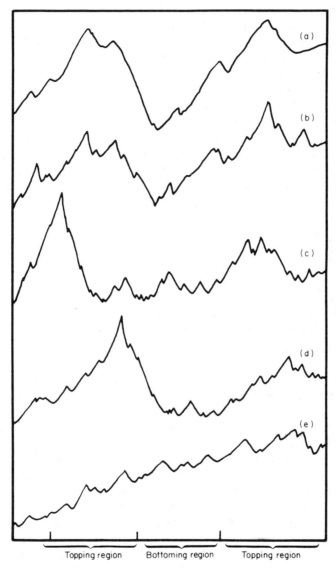

Figure 5.4. The share price movements of some hypothetical shares over a period of time: (a) an average for the market as a whole, (b) the movement of a fairly typical share, (c) an early topping share, (d) a late topping share, and (e) a 'rogue' share behaving contrariwise to the market.

exceptions are those few rogue shares travelling contrary to the market. This region can therefore be considered to be the region of the lowest risk for buying purposes. Conversely, the two regions which have been labelled as 'topping' regions are the regions of highest risk for buying. Shares in this region are either about to reach their peaks, and will soon be on their way down, or have already started to decline in price.

Although the rest of this chapter is going to be concerned with how to establish when we are at a market bottom, in order to buy shares, it can also be pointed out that, as far as selling is concerned, we should be aiming for the topping regions. if we miss these for any reason, then we should tend to hold on rather than sell at a bottom region because shares are then poised for an increase in price. However, if the rules outlined in the chapter on selling are adhered to closely, there will be no question of being caught holding shares in a declining market. We will be just about completely in cash, and probably hoping for a heavy fall in prices in order to buy back in at much cheaper levels.

TIMING OF MARKET TURNING POINTS

It is never possible to know at the time that the market has reached its lowest or highest value for the time being. If you rely on the financial press to inform you of the fact, you will be woefully wrong. If the market is in a falling phase, then on the day which later proves to have been the market bottom, the City pages will convince you that there is a long way to go yet, a further fall of 100 points is on the cards and the holocaust is just around the corner. On the other hand, when the market has been rising for some time, the press will be full of optimism, the index apparently has at least another 100 points rise in it, and all signals are at go. How, therefore, are we to reach any conclusion about the top or bottom of the market? The answer is that we can do this some time after the event. The later we are in deciding positively that such a day was the point at which the market turned upwards after its long fall, the more we are going to be scooped by investors who woke up to the fact before we did. Thus our potential for profit will be severely limited—in fact by the time commission etc. is taken into account, we may well end up with no profit. On the other hand, if we decide too soon that the market has turned up, and we make a large commitment, we may be wrong and suffer a loss of the capital which we have invested.

It is impossible to predict the stock market with any certainty, but we can learn from the lessons of the past. As we said earlier, we are most concerned with knowing when the market has passed its bottom, and is in a strong recovery, and conversely knowing when it has passed its peak and is on the way down. What we need is a system of rules that indicate, and have been successful in doing this in the past, when the market has turned. If we look again at the Index for the last 10 years or so, in Fig. 5.2 we can identify several points which may be called bottoms. They occurred in mid-1970, late 1974, late 1976, early 1979, late 1981, late 1983 and mid-1984. These are the points following which the greatest profits were to be made, since they were usually followed by spectacular rises of some 200 points or so in the Index. It was also still possible to make lesser profits out of less obvious bottoms, which were followed by more minor rises, such as those at the end of 1968, mid-1972, early 1973, mid-1975 and early 1978, late 1979, early 1981, even though these rises are for the most part superimposed on the downward part of a wave. Since these minor ripples are of much shorter duration than the waves, being of perhaps a few weeks' to a few months' duration, compared with a year or more for the waves, the timing of an investment to take advantage of these ripples is much more critical than timing of a wave. We can afford to lose a few weeks at the start of a new wave before we start to invest in selected shares, but to lose the same amount of time with a ripple introduces an unacceptable risk.

We can at this point define two types of investor. Firstly, the less aggressive type, who wishes to keep the risk involved with his investment down to a minimum; secondly, the aggressive investor, who is willing to take more risk in order to make larger profits. The first type should be prepared to take advantage of the waves, ignoring the minor ripples, while the second type of investor can consider using the ripples as a means of increasing his profit. Note that the aggressive investor will also make a larger profit out of waves, since the start of the wave appears as a ripple, triggering the aggressive investor into action, while the less aggressive investor waits a bit longer until he is sure that a large wave is in the process of formation.

These two types of investor are going to require two slightly different approaches or rules for timing a new investment, although both are based on the same system of plotting moving averages of the Friday closing values of the FT Index. Now it might be argued that since we have daily closing prices available to us we ought to be calculating and plotting data on a daily basis. To do this takes the investor of course five times as much effort as if he bases his decisions on weekly values, and the author's view on this is that daily calculations result in only a marginal improvement in investment performance when applied to buying and selling of shares. There are two areas, however, in which daily calculations are virtually essential, and that is in the currency market and the traded options market (see Chapter 10). Investors in the traded options market are vitally concerned with the high gearing to be obtained, and in that particular market moves of a few pennies in the underlying share price become magnified enormously in the option price. The very fine tuning of buying and selling operations essential for successful dealings in options can only be accomplished by daily study of the market.

MOVING AVERAGES

We have already pointed out earlier that a plot of the FT Index over the last 12 years consists of three trends, long term, medium term (waves) and short term (ripples). By a simple mathematical technique, which only depends upon the ability to add, subtract and divide, it is possible to separate the long term from the other trends, the medium term from the short term and weekly variations and the short term from the weekly variations. It is analogous to 'sandpapering' the overall graph in Fig. 5.2. By using a coarse sandpaper we would end up with a gently rising line, which would be the overall long-term trend. Using a medium-grade sandpaper, we would remove the jagged ripples, and be left with the waves of a couple of years or so duration. Finally, a fine sandpaper would remove the weekly variations and leave us with the short-term ripples.

Since our aim is to make profits within a realistic time span, rather than have to wait 5 years or so for them to mature, we will ignore long-term trends and concentrate upon medium- and short-term trends—the waves and ripples we have already mentioned. Thus we will only use medium and fine sandpaper on our graph. The fine sandpaper will be the calculation of a 5-week moving average, while the medium sandpaper will be a 13-week moving average of the FT Index weekly closing price. A 5-week average is what it says it is; the average value of the Index over the previous 5 weeks, and can be calculated by adding up the five values for the last 5 weeks and dividing by 5. Similarly, a 13-week average is calculated by adding up the values of the Index over the last 13 weeks and dividing by 13. The adjective 'moving' is in a sense superfluous, since all it means is that our average is changing each week, which it will normally do when we compare this week's value with last week's.

Rather than, each week, adding together the previous 13 weeks' values before we divide by 13, we can simplify things if we keep a note of the total for the previous 13 weeks before we divide it by 13. Then, the following week all we have to do is add the new week's value to this total, and subtract the value of the index of the 13-week average. A similar approach can be made to calculate the 5-week moving average, only this time we add the new week's value and subtract the 6th week back from the running total. The whole procedure should be clear from Table 5.2.

The total of the first 5-weeks' values of the FT Index is 4328.6 entered in the 5-week column. Divided by 5, this gives a 5-week average of 865.7. The next week the new value of 885.1 is added to this total, while the 6th week back value (870.0) is subtracted. This gives a new total of 4343.7

Table 5.2. Calculation of 5- and 13-week moving averages of the FT Index

Date	Index	5-week average			13-week average		
		Subtract	Total	Average	Subtract	Total	Average
21. 9.84	870.0	X			X		
28. 9.84	858.6	X			X		
5.10.84	866.2	X					
12.10.84	866.6	X					
19.10.84	867.2	X	4328.6	865.7			
26.10.84	885.1	X	4343.7	868.7			
2.11.84	907.6	X	4392.7	878.5			
9.11.84	900.1	X	4426.6	885.3			
16.11.84	920.0	X	4480.0	896.0			
23.11.84	910.3		4523.1	904.6			
30.11.84	917.3		4555.3	911.0			
7.12.84	923.0		4570.7	914.1			
14.12.84	935.4		4606.0	921.2		11 627.4	894.4
21.12.84	924.3		4610.3	922.0		11 681.7	898.6

which is divided by 5 to give a 5-week average of 868.7. In order to avoid confusion on which value is to be subtracted, we put a cross in the 'subtract' column opposite the value which we have just subtracted. Thus, the following week we know that the value following the one with a cross is the one to be subtracted.

We cannot compute a 13-week average, of course, until we have 13 weeks' values of the Index. Then we can proceed in the same way as we did for the 5-week average, but of course dividing the 13-week running totals by 13, and putting a cross in the 13-week 'subtract' column so as not to lose track of the value to be subtracted the following week.

After a time we will have list of values of the Index itself, the 5-week moving average and the 13-week moving average. We will be able to see at a glance whether the 5-week average and the 13-week average are both moving up, both moving down, or one going up and one going down. Although some people have the ability to extract a great deal of information from long columns of figures, it is easier to see what is going on, and has more impact, if these figures are plotted on a graph, since the various wave formations will then stand out clearly. To show the sandpapering effect of these moving averages on the weekly values of the index, separate graphs of the Index, the 5-week moving average and the 13-week moving average are shown in Fig. 5.5.

We now come to an important point about moving averages, which has frequently been ignored in books about share movements which have displayed such averages (usually a 200-day one) on top of graphs of weekly or daily prices. This point is that the average of a number of weekly prices has to be associated with the middle of the number of weeks taken. In the

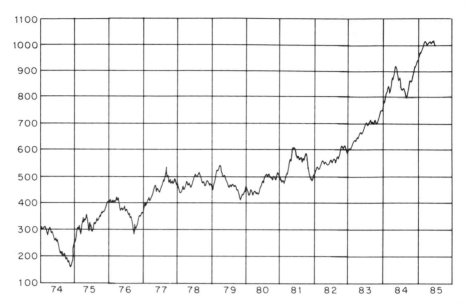

Figure 5.5. (a). The movements of the Financial Times Index weekly closing values since 1974. The Index is plotted on a linear scale.

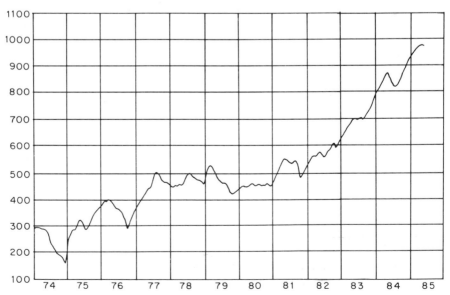

Figure 5.5. (b). The 5-week moving average of the weekly closing values of the Financial Times Index since 1974.

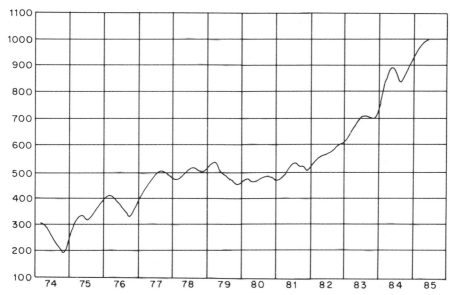

Figure 5.5. (c). The 13-week moving average of the weekly closing values of the Financial Times Index since 1974.

table which earlier showed how to calculate these averages, we put the values for both the 5-week and 13-week averages opposite the last weekly price that we had used. This is perfectly fine if we are just using the table to tell us when the average has changed from a down direction to an up direction, but we cannot put these three values—weekly, 5-week average and 13-week average—on the same week's position on a graph. So, the 5-week average has to be plotted 3 weeks back in time, i.e. the middle week of the 5-week span, and the 13-week average has to be plotted 7 weeks back, the middle of a 13-week span. Fig. 5.6 shows the three graphs from Fig. 5.5 displayed on the same grid. For the reasons we have been discussing, the 5-week average terminates 3 weeks before, and the 13-week average 7 weeks before the end of the weekly price points. Figure 5.5 emphasizes an aspect that is lost if the averages are not plotted with this time lag—the weekly price oscillates about the 5-week average, which in turn oscillates about the 13-week average. As we will discuss in the final chapter, the larger the number of weeks used to compute an average, the smoother the resulting curve will be and the easier it will be to predict it forward into the future. Knowing that these various averages oscillate about each other makes it easier to predict price ranges for shares and so correctly plotted moving averages have a very useful predictive value.

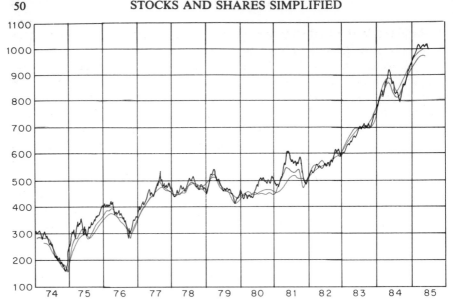

Figure 5.6. The relationship between the weekly closing values of the Financial Times Index (black), the 5-week moving average (green) and the 13-week moving average (red).

In order to avoid confusion we shall continue to calculate the averages exactly as shown in Table 5.2, since in this chapter we are almost exclusively interested in when the averages signal that they have changed direction; which we interpret as meaning the market has changed direction. Whenever the averages are plotted on a graph, however, they will always be plotted with the appropriate time-lag. Thus when we want, for historical reasons, to retrieve from a graph of moving averages the actual dates when at the time we would have seen the average change direction, we have to add the appropriate time-lag to the date the averages reached a maximum or minimum on the graph.

Now, the question is, how are these moving averages going to help us to decide that it is time to make an investment? The answer is most clearly illustrated by reference to the graph of the 13-week moving average. There are fifteen points at which the average changes direction from down to up, and these occur in early 1975; late 1975; late 1976; mid-1978; early 1979; twice in early 1980; early 1981; mid-1981; late 1981; late 1982; early, mid, late 1983 and mid-1984. If you look at the same points on the more complex graph of the Index itself, you can see that the Index usually then rose by very large amounts, of the order of 100 or 200 points, except for the points in early 1980 and mid-1981. So a turn-up in 13-week moving average has, in the recent past, acted as a signal to us to tell us that in all probability a considerable rise in the market has just started, and that it is time for us to get invested in order to take advantage of the coming rise.

Well, what about the 5-week average? A closer look at its picture shows that the 5-week average has also changed from down to up at about the same points the 13-week average did, but that in addition it also turned up on several other occasions for short periods when the 13-week average did not. In other words, the 5-week average can give a false signal that the market is changing over to a strong upward trend. If you look at these times of a false signal on the graph of the Index itself, it will be noticed that even so, there was still a small rise in the Index, which usually only lasted a few weeks, but this is still enough either to make a small profit or to limit the loss to a small one provided one is prepared to sell out a few weeks later when it becomes obvious that the signal is false because the 13-week average does not turn up.

It is difficult to see, because of the large time-scale in Fig. 5.5, the small time differences between a turn-up in the Index itself, a turn-up in the 5-week average and a turn-up in the 13-week average. In order to get over this problem, Table 5.3 shows these three values for a few weeks either side of the turning points mentioned earlier in 1975, 1976, 1978, 1979, 1980, 1981, 1982, 1983 and 1984.

From the figures in Table 5.3 it can be seen that the 5-week average is more volatile than the 13-week average; that is, it reacts more quickly than the latter to a change in the direction of the market from falling to rising. For example, in the market bottom during December 1974/January 1975, the lowest value of the weekly index was achieved on 27th December. The 5-week average turned up on 10th January, and the 13-week average turned up 2 weeks later on 24th January. The Index itself rose some 80 points between 17th and 24th January, and then a further 100 points or so during the next few months. So an investor who jumped the gun and invested when the 5-week average turned up on 10th January made a considerably larger profit than one who waited 2 weeks longer.

Sometimes there is a gap of several weeks between the turning up of the 5-week average and the 13-week average. The market bottom which occurred in October/November 1976 is a case in point. From Table 5.3 it can be seen that the Index reached its lowest point on 29th October and the 5-week average turned up 2 weeks later, on 12th November. It was not until 31st December that the 13-week index turned up. The Index itself climbed about 60 points during the period between the two signals. There was still plenty of profit left in the situation, because by the following September the Index climbed to a then record high of just short of 550.

The two averages of the FT Index and the Index itself are plotted on graphs for each of these five bottoms in Figure 5.6. We can see how the bottoms in the Index and in each of the two averages now almost overlap,

Table 5.3. Behaviour of weekly closing values of the FT Index and the 5-week and 13-week moving averages of weekly closing values of the Index at major market bottoms

Market Bottom	Date	FT Index*	5-week average	13-week average
December 1974/	29 Nov. 74	165	175	190
January 1975	6 Dec. 74	160	168	185
	13 Dec. 74	150	162	181
	20 Dec. 74	161	160	179
	27 Dec. 74	147	157	176
	3 Jan. 75	150	154	173
	10 Jan. 75	175	157	170
	17 Jan. 75	170	161	168
	24 Jan. 75	252	179	172
	31 Jan. 75	230	195	175
	7 Feb. 75	275	220	182
August 1975	11 July 75	330	316	333
	18 July 75	296	307	329
	25 July 75	285	298	325
	1 Aug. 75	290	298	325
	8 Aug. 75	287	298	320
	15 Aug. 75	280	288	316
	22 Aug. 75	295	287	312
	29 Aug. 75	310	292	309
	5 Sept. 75	326	300	306
	12 Sept. 75	318	306	304
	19 Sept. 75	343	318	305
October 1976	1 Oct. 76	322	341	361
	8 Oct. 76	287	328	353
	15 Oct. 76	305	321	346
	22 Oct. 76	285	310	339
	29 Oct. 76	264	293	331
	5 Nov. 76	281	284	324
	12 Nov. 76	308	289	319
	19 Nov. 76	318	291	316
	26 Nov. 76	294	293	311
	3 Dec. 76	295	299	307
	10 Dec. 76	324	308	306
	17 Dec. 76	331	312	305
	24 Dec. 76	345	318	305
	31 Dec. 76	365	332	308
March 1978	3 Feb. 78	471	483	478
	10 Feb. 78	456	474	477
	17 Feb. 78	459	470	477
	24 Feb. 78	445	462	474
	3 Mar. 78	436	453	471
	10 Mar. 78	459	451	469
	17 Mar. 78	451	450	468
	24 Mar. 78	461	450	467
	31 Mar. 78	464	454	465
	7 Apr. 78	467	460	463
	14 Apr. 78	447	458	460

Table 5.3. *(Continued)*

Market Bottom	Date	FT Index*	5-week average	13-week average
	21 Apr. 78	454	459	457
	28 Apr. 78	466	460	457
	5 May 78	482	463	457
	12 May 78	488	467	460
February 1979	19 Jan. 79	479	476	479
	26 Jan. 79	465	474	477
	2 Feb. 79	467	473	476
	9 Feb. 79	451	467	475
	16 Feb. 79	455	463	473
	23 Feb. 79	461	460	472
	2 Mar. 79	485	464	472
	9 Mar. 79	515	473	474
	16 Mar. 79	511	485	476
	23 Mar. 79	535	501	480
May 1980	2 May 80	443	436	444
	9 May 80	437	437	442
	16 May 80	436	437	440
	23 May 80	423	433	438
	30 May 80	416	431	434
	6 June 80	429	428	432
	13 June 80	457	432	433
	20 June 80	472	439	436
	27 June 80	464	447	439
January 1981	2 Jan. 81	475	468	481
	9 Jan. 81	461	466	481
	16 Jan. 81	452	464	478
	23 Jan. 81	456	462	475
	30 Jan. 81	466	462	474
	6 Feb. 81	480	463	474
	13 Feb. 81	493	469	474
	20 Feb. 81	488	477	472
	27 Feb. 81	507	487	473
	6 Mar. 81	489	492	474
	13 Mar. 81	477	491	475
October 1981	2 Oct. 81	476	515	532
	9 Oct. 81	498	504	530
	16 Oct. 81	463	486	525
	23 Oct. 81	462	475	521
	30 Oct. 81	469	474	516
	6 Nov. 81	495	477	513
	13 Nov. 81	519	481	509
	20 Nov. 81	520	493	506
	27 Nov. 81	533	507	503
	4 Dec. 81	529	519	501
	11 Dec. 81	520	524	498
	18 Dec. 81	521	525	499
	25 Dec. 81	519	525	502

Continued

Table 5.3. *(Continued)*

Market Bottom	Date	FT Index*	5-week average	13-week average
July 1982	2 July 82	543	564	569
	9 July 82	553	657	568
	16 July 82	557	552	569
	23 July 82	557	552	568
	30 July 82	557	553	567
	6 Aug. 82	549	554	564
	13 Aug. 82	545	553	560
	20 Aug. 82	581	557	562
	27 Aug. 82	574	561	561
	3 Sept. 82	596	569	562
	10 Sept. 82	575	574	561
	17 Sept. 82	564	578	561
	24 Sept. 82	582	578	564
September 1983	9 Sept. 83	696	717	712
	16 Sept. 83	705	711	710
	23 Sept. 83	694	705	708
	30 Sept. 83	708	704	710
	7 Oct. 83	698	700	711
	14 Oct. 83	678	697	709
	21 Oct. 83	689	694	707
	28 Oct. 83	706	696	707
	4 Nov. 83	720	698	706
	11 Nov. 83	727	704	706
	18 Nov. 83	726	714	706
	25 Nov. 83	747	725	708
July 1984	6 July 84	793	817	851
	13 July 84	771	804	842
	20 July 84	764	790	834
	27 July 84	791	786	824
	3 Aug. 84	831	790	818
	10 Aug. 84	850	801	816
	17 Aug. 84	840	815	815
	24 Aug. 84	832	829	815
	31 Aug. 84	838	838	815
	7 Sept. 84	858	845	817

* To nearest whole number

and it is also evident that the weekly index values oscillate about the averages.

The dates at which the 5-week averages and 13-week averages signalled a rise in the market are given in Table 5.4. As we have mentioned, since the beginning of 1974 the 13-week average has changed direction from down to up 15 times, and for 10 of these points the market has shown a considerable rise, while for one further point a moderate rise occurred. In fact, we could go back even further to the end of the war in 1945 and the same thing is

Table 5.4. Market rises signalled by 5-week and 13-week averages since 1974 and whether correct or not

5-week average signals			13-week average signals		
	1974			1974	
3 May		wrong	none		
26 July		wrong			
25 Oct.		wrong			
	1975			1975	
10 Jan.		right	24 Jan.		right
4 Apr.		wrong	19 Sept.		right
29 Aug.		right			
	1976			1976	
2 July		wrong	31 Dec.		right
12 Nov.		right			
	1977			1977	
5 Aug.		right	none		
23 Dec.		right			
	1978			1978	
24 Feb.		right	5 May		right
28 Apr.		right			
14 July		right			
8 Dec.		wrong			
	1979			1979	
2 Mar.		right	9 Mar.		right
17 Aug.		wrong			
21 Sept.		wrong			
14 Dec.		wrong			
	1980			1980	
13 June		right	25 Jan.		wrong
24 Oct.		wrong	14 Nov.		wrong
	1981			1981	
6 Feb.		right	27 Feb.		right
3 July		wrong	14 Aug.		wrong
14 Aug.		wrong	18 Dec.		right
6 Nov.		right			
	1982			1982	
20 Aug.		right	3 Sept.		right
	1983			1983	
14 Jan.		right	28 Jan.		right
20 May		wrong	15 July		wrong
5 Aug.		wrong	18 Nov.		right
28 Oct.		right			
	1984			1984	
2 Mar.		right	24 Aug.		right
3 Aug.		right			

true about the 13-week average, i.e. that on the great majority of occasions there has been a good market rise. We can conclude therefore that in future any turn-up in the 13-week average has a high probability of being correct in signalling a considerable rise in share prices.

There is no such high probability attached to a change from down to up in the direction of the 5-week moving average, as can be seen from Table 5.4. Of 31 signals given between the beginning of 1974 and September 1979, 17 were correct and 14 were incorrect. On these occasions where change in the 5-week average has been a correct signal for a market rise, confirmed by a turn-up in the 13-week average, the great advantage of it has been the earlier opportunity to get into the market. We can see from Table 5.4 that on such occasions the turn-up in the 5-week average precedes that in the 13-week average by anything from 1 to 6 weeks.

Since, as has been pointed out, the 5-week moving average sometimes gives a false signal, in the sense that the market does then not move upwards for a lengthy period but only for a few weeks, then it will be more appropriate for an aggressive investor to take advantage of such a situation, while the less aggressive investor is more temperamentally suited to waiting until the bull market is confirmed by the 13-week average. It is important to decide into what category you should put yourself.

AGGRESSIVE AND CAUTIOUS INVESTORS

By definition, the cautious investor is a person who is less willing to take risks than an aggressive investor. He will take a bit more time to be convinced that the market is moving ahead, and that it is time to buy his selected shares. Because of this longer period of time necessary to take an investment decision, he will necessarily make less profit out of the changed condition of the market than an aggressive investor who has acted a few weeks earlier. He will have to pay higher prices for his shares because prices will have been moving ahead during those crucial weeks. On the other hand, the more cautious investor may score on those occasions when the market has given a false indication that it has changed direction for the better. He is able to stand back and watch his more adventurous colleagues take losses, unless they are prepared to admit to themselves that they have made a mistake and decide to close out their positions.

It is important to know yourself psychologically, since to act aggressively when one is fundamentally cautious can lead to a number of sleepless nights worrying about the size of the commitment you have made. Investment under these conditions ceases to be the source of pleasure it ought to be and becomes a source of tension. There is even a category of people who worry unduly even when following the rules outlined for the more cautious investor. Such people should avoid the stock market entirely and concentrate upon the other forms of investment discussed in the opening chapter of this book. As a general rule, at least until one has gained more experience in investment, if a particular holding becomes a source of worry it should be reduced to levels at which you can come to terms with the uncertainty. If you cannot do this, it is probably best to close out the entire holding in that security.

A further point at which individual investor psychology comes into play is in selling a particular holding, especially if it has only been held for a short time. Some investors consider that to sell is some sort of confession of failure. Nothing could be further from the truth. A decision to buy is based upon all the knowledge available at the time of buying. Conditions may well change a week later for that particular security so that it then becomes a bad holding. To sell then is not a confession of failure, but an indication that you have been alert to the changed circumstances and their implication for your particular holding. The fact to bear in mind at all times is that your capital has been hard come by, and that your aim is to increase it or preserve it. Cutting adrift from a losing situation may not increase your capital but is certainly preserving it for investment elsewhere under more favourable conditions.

The Cautious Investor

The key to investment decisions by a cautious investor will be the movement of the 13-week moving average. Once this turns up from its downward trend the probability is that we can look forward to many months of a steadily rising market and, provided the correct choice of shares has been made, a large increase in capital will occur. It is essential to become fully invested within a few weeks of this turn-up in the 13-week average, otherwise the largest slice of profits, which normally occurs at the beginning of a new bull market, will be missed. As discussed later, the choice of investments will have usually narrowed itself down to about four or five shares, since to be invested in more results in too thin a spread, with possible reduction in profits, as well as being difficult to keep fully abreast of at all times.

There is something to be said for spreading the investment in each particular share over a period of 2 or 3 weeks, buying, say, one-third of the envisaged holding at a time, and not buying the next third until the price has moved up. This, of course, results in an average price for the share that is higher than if the complete holding had been bought at the beginning, but as long as the price is rising during the period, this average price will be less than the market price. This means that at all times there will be a profit locked into the situation, which hopefully will not be allowed to trickle away. If the price does not rise shortly after the initial investment, due to unforeseen circumstances, we then have two-thirds of the anticipated sum left to invest in our other choices which should be doing much better.

Although the turn-up in the 13-week moving average is the trigger for the cautious investor, the 5-week average can be used as an early-warning device that the 13-week average may shortly move upward. Thus he should be following both averages closely and as soon as the 5-week turns up he can finalize his choice of shares in readiness for the change in direction of the 13-week moving average, should it occur.

The Aggressive Investor

The aggressive investor is willing to increase the risk inherent in making an investment in order to increase his profits. Thus he needs a signal which is more volatile than the 13-week average and tells him more quickly than the latter that the bottom of the market has probably been passed, but with less certainty than the signal from the 13-week average (certainty is less because something has to be traded for the gain in time). The 5-week moving average fulfils the requirement of the agressive investor, but, as mentioned before, and as can be seen from the plot of the 5-week average in Figs 5.5 and 5.6, there are a number of occasions when this average turns up only for a short time and is not followed by the 13-week average.

Both the correct and incorrect signals of the 5-week moving average have already been given in Table 5.4, where we showed that there were 17 correct and 14 incorrect signals. Therefore there is not much better than an even chance that a turn-up in the 5-week average is indicating the start of a bull market. This may appear to be something of a gamble, but several points should be borne in mind. Firstly, even if the indication is false, there may be an opportunity to make a small profit by selling a week or so after buying, because prices will rise for a short time, at least in those securities which have been chosen because of their potential gain. Secondly, if a profit is not forthcoming, the loss should be minimal provided the position is sold out when it is realized that a bull market is not commencing. Thirdly, although the chances of the 5-week average indicating the start of a bull market are about evens, the chances of a profit are very much greater than this, since if it is the start of a new bull market, the profits are going to be very large indeed, whereas if it is not, the loss will be small, being limited by the fact that you sell out. The professionals may well use the terms 'upside potential' and 'downside potential' in this situation. When the 5-week moving average turns up, the upside potential is greater than the downside potential.

It must be emphasized again, however, that this is only true if the aggressive investor is prepared to recognize that he may well have to sell a holding shortly after he has acquired it if the market has given a false indication. Failure to do this may result in such losses that a good proportion of the rise during the eventual bull market will be offset by them.

The rules discussed above can be restated simply as follows:

1. While the 5-week and 13-week moving averages are falling, do not buy shares.
2. When the 5-week average turns up, with the 13-week average falling, the aggressive investor can buy, but be prepared to sell soon if the 5-week average turns down again and the 13-week average continues to fall.
3. When the 13-week average turns up the cautious investor can now buy within the next few weeks. The aggressive investor now knows he was right.

Chapter 6

What to Buy

The next most important decision after deciding when to buy is what to buy, and this chapter is concerned with the development of selection procedures. Although, eventually, certain shares are recommended for buying, the recommendation or otherwise of shares does not imply praise or criticism of those companies or the way in which the companies are managed. The selections are based entirely on the movement of the share prices.

As pointed out in the last chapter, when the market turns up in a new bull phase, almost all equities rise in value. So, provided we have a reasonable spread of investments in our portfolio, our portfolio will also gain. It is correct timing that virtually guarantees a profit. The size of the profit, however, will depend upon which equities we have bought. A badly selected portfolio may appreciate by only a few per cent during a roaring bull market, and nothing is more galling than to see your shares left behind in the general stampede upwards. On the other hand, a properly selected portfolio will be at the front of the stampede, and you may easily see the value of your holding double in the course of a few months.

The magnitude of the problem in choosing shares to buy is easily grasped by a quick glance at the back pages of the *Financial Times*. The list of equities quoted on the London Stock Exchange covers nearly two whole pages, 12 columns in all. So, how are we to select the winners from this bewildering variety of shares? One way of looking at this problem might be to decide that somebody, somewhere, in the past has already reduced this large list down to 30 shares in the form of the 'blue chip' companies which form the FT30 Index. After all, these are considered to be the backbone of British industry, and so we would think that we cannot go far wrong by investing in these. In support of this approach is the fact that, in the last chapter, we showed that we could determine, with a high probability, the point in time at which the Index, i.e. these 30 companies, would show a large rise of the order of 100 to 200 points. Although 'buying the Index' is a feasible proposition, we can put forward a number of good reasons for not adopting this approach to investment in equities.

The first of these is the large cost, as far as the small private investor is concerned. The smallest investment in each share is going to be of the order of £200 to £400, if buying costs are to be kept to a reasonable minimum. Because of this, only investors who can splash out £6000 to £12 000 are in a position to undertake this exercise.

A second reason is the difficulty in giving the amount of attention to such a large portfolio that is necessary if it is to be managed properly. All through this book, the theme is that investment should not be an onerous task, and that a portfolio of not more than six shares is probably the best size for the person with limited spare time available. With 30 shares to follow each week it would be difficult to reach clear-headed decisions about selling individual holdings when it is necessary to do so. There will be a tendency to allow longer and longer time intervals to elapse between evaluations of the situation. As shown in the next chapter, this can be an expensive failing, since prices, even of blue chip companies, can fall dramatically in the course of a week or two.

A third factor, which is very important, and perhaps not so obvious, is that the profit potential of the Index itself is fairly limited. Even in a roaring bull phase the Index is unlikely to rise by more than 20–30%. Although a 100-point rise looks spectacular, percentage-wise it only represents 20% if it occurs when the Index is already at 500, and 10% at the levels of the Index at the time of writing. Of course, as pointed out earlier, because of the way in which it is constructed, the constituents of the Index do slightly better than the Index itself; even so, this only makes a small difference and the fact remains that we are unlikely to make large profits out of these 30 companies. It is, of course, important to make large profits when the Index is rising, because these have to make up for those other occasions when the market is falling, and we are not invested.

The first edition of this book discussed the gains that would have been made by an investor buying the shares of the FT30 Index on 5th May 1978, which was a point where the 5-week moving average turned upwards following a major market turning point. The most recent market turning point at the time of writing was July/August 1984, and the 5-week moving average turned up on this occasion on 3rd August 1984, and so for comparison we can also see what happened to the shares of the FT30 Index between this point and May 1985.

Taking the 1978 market first of all, the 5-week average of the FT30 Index signalled a market rise on 5th May 1978. The Index itself ended the week at 481.5. One year later, the day after the General Election, the Index reached a then all-time high of 558.6 on 4th May 1979. The gain in the Index

Table 6.1. Price movement of the shares of the FT30 constituent companies during the year 5 May 78 to 4 May 79

Share	Price at 5 May 78	Price at 4 May 79	Percentage gain (loss)	Share	Price at 5 May 78	Price at 4 May 79	Percentage gain (loss)
Allied Brew.	93.5	102	9.1	Grand Met.	113	179	58.4
Beecham	664	725	9.2	GKN	284	308	8.5
Blue Circle	252	342	35.7	Hawker	214	266	24.3
BOC	75	81	8.0	ICI	358	414	15.6
Boots	210	235	11.9	Imperial	79.5	107	34.6
Bowater	203	209	3.0	London Br.	70	72	2.9
BP	824	1230	49.3	Lucas	300	310	3.3
J. Brown	324	587	81.2	M & S	147	130	(11.6)
Cad. Schwep.	53	69	30.2	P & O	99	86	(13.1)
Courtaulds	124	116	(6.5)	Plessey	98	107	9.2
Distillers	186	249	33.9	Tate & Lyle	190	156	(17.9)
Dunlop	81	80	(1.2)	Tube Inv.	374	436	16.6
EMI	144	114	(20.8)	Turner & N	176	166	(5.7)
GEC	253	450	77.9	UDS	94	121	28.7
Glaxo	565	515	(8.8)	Vickers	182	210	15.4

Average gain 16.0%

over the year was therefore 16%. Table 6.1 shows the prices of the shares of the constituent companies on those dates and the percentage gain (or loss) of these during the period. The gain in these companies' shares over the year was also 16.0%.

In the 1984 market, the 5-week moving average signalled a rise in the market on 3rd August 1984. The Index at that point was 830.5, and at the time of writing (24th May 1985) the Index finished the week at 1001.6, with a gain therefore of 20.6% over the period. Table 6.2 shows the prices of the shares at the two relevant dates along with the percentage gain or loss during the period. The average gain in the 30 companies' shares was 30% over the period. Note that of course British Telecom did not come to market until December 1984, so the starting price entered for that is the price at the launch, i.e. 105p.

An alternative to investing in all 30 of these companies is, of course, to select just six or less of their number. This would overcome the objections of the large cost involved in buying into all 30, and would also give us a portfolio of manageable size. The problem is, unfortunately, that we have no means of deciding which of the 30 are going to do best during the following year. We may, through good luck or judgement, happen upon the six which do best, which in the case of those in Table 6.1 would have been John Brown, GEC, Grand Metropolitan, British Petroleum, Blue Circle Cement and Imperial Group. This would have made us an average gain of 56.2% over the year. In the case of those shares listed in Table 6.2, the best six performers were BTR, Blue Circle, Hanson, Lucas and Vickers. The average gain from these would have been 70.5% over the period.

On the other hand, of course, we might through bad luck just pick on the worst performers, which in Table 6.1 would have been EMI, P & O, Marks & Spencer, Glaxo, Tate & Lyle and Courtaulds. In such a case we would have made an average loss of 13.1% during the year. In fact, since eight of the 30 shares actually declined during 1978/9, there is about a one in four chance that any share picked at random would be a loser among any six selected at random. As far as the 1984 selection is concerned, the worst performers would have been Associated Dairies, Distillers, GEC, Grand Metropolitan and Plessey, with an average loss of 4.2% for the period.

Having decided that investing in all, or just a few of the shares of the companies comprising the FT Index is either too big a task, or unlikely to yield us a large profit, then we have to find some other way of selecting shares. Of course, this other way has to be an improvement on the FT30 list, otherwise we would be better off, in spite of the disadvantages just pointed out, in investing in a small number of shares chosen from the FT30 constituents. So, each time we reduce the list of shares down from the initial number as listed on the back pages of the *Financial Times*, we will have to

Table 6.2. Price movement of the shares of the FT30 constituent companies from 3 Aug. 1984 to 24 May 1985

Share	Price at 3 Aug. 84	Price at 24 May 85	Percentage gain (loss)	Share	Price at 3 Aug. 84	Price at 24 May 85	Percentage gain (loss)
All. Lyons	151	192	27.1	Glaxo	840	1250	48.8
As. Dair.	146	152	4.1	Grand Met.	294	298	1.4
BP	428	530	23.8	Hawker	409	435	6.4
BICC	210	228	8.6	ICI	548	752	37.2
BTR	210	363	72.9	Imperial	141	189	34.0
Beecham	290	355	22.4	Hanson	142	228	60.6
Blue Circle	355	533	50.1	Lucas	170	301	77.1
BOC	240	299	24.6	M & S	109	137	25.7
Boots	154	184	19.5	Nat. West	490	668	36.2
Br. Telecom	105*	154	46.7	P & O	303	368	21.5
Cad. Schwep.	118	157	33.1	Plessey	198	150	(24.2)
Courtaulds	110	145	31.8	Tate & Lyle	322	450	39.8
Distillers	289	288	(0.3)	Thorn—EMI	400	457	14.3
GEC	186	182	(2.1)	THF	106	137	29.2
GKN	164	226	37.8	Vickers	168	322	91.7
						Average gain	30.0%

*British Telecom commenced trading Dec. 1984

check that the performance of the reduced list is superior to that of the FT30 companies.

The most obvious way of choosing shares is by selecting them at random from all those possible. This could be done by, for example, throwing 30 darts at the relevant pages of the *Financial Times*. This may sound foolish but the interesting point emerges that in 1978 we would have done better by doing this than by investing in some or all of the FT30 shares. This is because, perhaps surprisingly, the constituents of the FT30 Index did not perform as well as the whole market during the year commencing 5th May 1978. We have already pointed out that the FT Index rose from 481.5 to 558.6, a gain of 16%, while the constituents' shares also gained 17.3%. The All Share Index, covering 750 shares, rose from 216.68 to 283.82 during the year, for a gain of 31.2%. Things were not quite the same from the August 1984 low point, since the All Share Index rose from 499.14 to 634.53, a gain of 27.1%. In this case the constituent companies of the FT30 Index slightly outperformed the All Share Index.

There are a number of criteria we can apply to shorten the large number of shares down to manageable proportions, but each time we apply such a selection procedure it has to result in an improved gain over the year for our shorter list. If we were selecting shares for their performance since May 1978, therefore, we must end up with a list with a gain of better than the whole market's gain of 31.2%. A further point about the selection procedures is that they should be fairly simple to carry out, and the simplest would be based entirely upon considerations of the movements in the share prices themselves. We want simplicity because, as we have pointed out before, we have to make the whole business of investment fairly undemanding in terms of our time. If we are going to consider company profits, the latest news about particular companies, and other types of fundamental data, we will soon be swamped with the demands of keeping up with this vast amount of information. If we are able to demonstrate that we can achieve good results just from a consideration of the share prices, without having to keep up with all the other data, then we can accept this as being a satisfactory situation in terms of the return for our effort. Having decided upon a method that worked for the 1978 market, we also need to check that it has worked for subsequent markets, and the obvious way of testing this, of course, is to apply exactly the same procedures to the market at the latest turning point in August 1984.

We can put forward, at least as a start, two criteria which would, superficially, appear sensible ways of spotlighting those shares which we can expect to do well. We can then test each of these criteria for effectiveness, as discussed above, in choosing shares which outperform the rest of the market.

1. Larger profits can be made out of shares which have a history of fluctuating widely in price, i.e. which can be considered to be volatile shares.
2. Larger profits can be made out of shares which have not declined as
   much as the market in general prior to the start of the latest bull market.

VOLATILE SHARES

As far as volatility is concerned, it would seem obvious that, if we are after
a large profit, it makes no sense to invest in shares whose price historically
has moved within a narrow range. On the other hand, shares which move
over a wide range each year have the potential to make us large profits. The
pessimist may well argue that they have the potential to make us a large loss,
which is of course true if one neglects proper timing of the investment.
Provided we buy at the correct time, which can be determined as we showed
in the last chapter, the risk of loss is minimized. An actual example would
serve to show the potential for profit by investing in such a share. The yearly
price ranges for the engineering company Babcock & Wilcox Ltd (now
called Babcock International) are shown in Fig. 6.1. Before going into
detail, some general comments can be made about the presentation of share
charts. The price scale on such charts is almost always presented as a
logarithmic scale, rather than the linear scale such as we used in displaying
movements in the FT 30 Index. These scales have the property that a
percentage change in the price covers the same vertical distance irrespective
of the starting price. Thus the distance between 20p and 40p is the same as
the distance between 30p and 60p (100% increase in both instances). This
would not be true of course for a linear scale, the distance between 30p and
60p being half as much again as that between 20p and 40p. Where we are
interested in profit, which is best expressed as a percentage, we can more
easily gauge this from a logarithmic chart than a linear one, but for a
prediction of price movements a linear scale is usually advantageous. Hence
both are used in this book, depending on the aspect of investment being
discussed.

   In the case of Babcock & Wilcox, the logarithmic scale means that bars
of the same length would indicate the same percentage change or degree of
volatility. It can be seen that the length of the bars, and hence the volatility,
has tended to increase since the late 1960s, implying that Babcock & Wilcox
shares are now fluctuating each year more widely than previously. Of
course, this tendency may well reverse in the future.

   Although the advantage of such a chart is in its simplicity in depicting
price ranges, we must not be misled into thinking that such an amount of
profit is available each year. This is because the chart does not show when
the extremes of the price range were reached. To see that, one has to look
at a chart of the weekly closing prices over a period of time. Such a chart

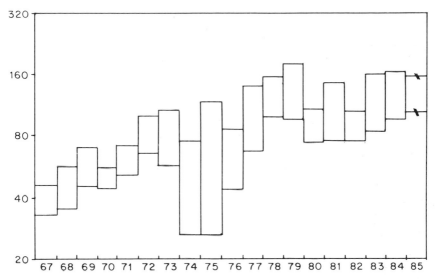

Figure 6.1. Yearly price ranges of shares of Babcock since 1967. Prices are on a logarithmic scale.

for Babcock & Wilcox is given in Chapter 7. The shares may well have started the year at a high and ended the year at a low. In a sense, therefore, the chart also shows the potential for loss as well as profit. What is obvious from the chart is that usually the high for each year has always been higher than the low for the preceding year. So, even if we neglect the fact that for about half of the years shown in Fig. 6.1 it would be possible to buy at the low and sell at the high within the same year, we can look at the less advantageous case of buying at one year's low and selling at the following year's high just to gain some idea of the possible profit. If we were able to buy exactly at the highs and lows, we would achieve a very large profit, as shown in Table 6.3.

A person who started with £100 invested in Babcock & Wilcox in 1967, and continued to buy and sell, reinvesting the proceeds at the exact lows and highs, would have ended with an investment worth £14 490 in 1984! As pointed out above, the actual gain would have been many times higher than this because extra transactions could have been carried out in some of the in-between years where the low preceded the high.

Of course, the above calculation is theoretical, because no-one is going to be able to buy exactly at the bottom and sell exactly at the top consistently. What we can hope for, however, is that we can get fairly near to those positions, say within 5 or 10% of the lows and highs.

It should be pointed out that, because of this difficulty of determining the exact points of the highs and lows in share prices, we will make almost no

Table 6.3. The results of transactions in Babcock & Wilcox shares since 1967 at peak highs and lows

Year bought	Year sold	Price bought	Price sold	Percentage gain
1967	1968	34	59	73
1969	1970	48	59.5	23
1971	1972	55.5	105.5	90
1973	1974	60	74	23
1975	1976	25	92	268
1977	1978	70	165	135
1979	1980	100	116	16
1981	1982	78	110	41
1983	1984	86	178	106

Cumulative gain 14 390

profit out of buying and selling shares which only move 20% or so between their low and high point. For example, if a share fluctuates between a low price of 150p and a high price of 180p, i.e. a gain of 20%, then being realistic, we are unlikely to buy at better than 155 to 160p and sell at 170 to 175p. Thus our profit, excluding buying and selling costs, will only be of the order of 10 to 20p, which is about 7 to 14% depending upon the exact prices involved. If we carry out the 'round trip' of buying and selling over a short period of time so that no dividend is received to offset commissions, etc., then our profit will be of the order of 0 to 7% or so. Because of this, it is crucial to deal in shares which are going to swing much more than 20% between their highs and lows.

To show how this real-life situation would change the theoretical gains given in Table 6.3, we can make the assumption that we can get to within 10% of the buying and selling prices of Babcock & Wilcox. So, the buying

Table 6.4. The results of transactions in Babcock & Wilcox shares since 1967 at probable buying and selling prices

Year bought	Year sold	Price bought	Price sold	Percentage gain
1967	1968	37	53	43
1969	1970	53	53	0
1971	1972	61	95	56
1973	1974	66	67	1
1975	1976	28	83	196
1977	1978	77	149	93
1979	1980	110	104	− 5
1981	1982	86	99	15
1983	1984	95	160	68

Cumulative gain 2262

and selling prices at which we would probably have bought, and the resulting profits, are given in Table 6.4.

The cumulative gain of 2262% obtained by buying and selling nine times since 1967 is high by any standards, and represents an average gain of about 52% per transaction, reinforcing the case for investing in volatile shares.

Since we are advocating the purchase of volatile shares, we may well ask how volatile UK shares are on the whole. This can be gauged from Fig. 6.2, in which the percentage movements from their low values are given for 500 shares in 1978. These shares were chosen on a random basis, so that they give a fair representation of the market as a whole. It can be seen that very few shares moved less than 20% from their low values, and very few moved more than about 160%. There were some extremely volatile shares which moved between a factor of five and ten times their low values, but since these are few and atypical, they are not shown on the figure. The 'average' share showed a movement of between 20 and 50% from its low value during the year, so that we can define volatile shares for our purposes as being shares which moved more than the average, say 70% and upwards.

Having shown the advantage possible when investing in a volatile share, it now remains to be shown that in general such shares are going to give a better result than the market as a whole. We can do this by considering a list of such shares based upon their highs and lows for the preceding year, the list being constructed during the early part of 1978, a time when the market in general was falling. The downward trend of the market was confirmed by the fact that the 5-week and 13-week moving averages of the FT Index were both falling.

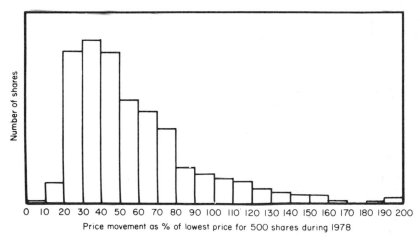

Figure 6.2. Volatility of UK shares. The histogram, derived from a total of 500 shares, shows the number of shares in categories of movements from under 10 to 200%.

The list of shares given in Table 6.5, 118 in all, was chosen so as to be fairly representative in numbers of the various sectors of the market, such as electrical, engineering, food etc. The high and low values for the previous year at the time of compilation of the list are given under the heading '1977/78 low, high'. The volatility of the shares is represented by the ratio of the high to the low price for the year 1977/78. In this table, the least volatile share is Grand Metropolitan, with a high/low ratio of 1.76, while the most volatile is Automated Security, with a ratio of 10.7. Since the buy signal was given during the first week in May 1978, the price of these shares is given on 5th May 1978, and the price on 4th May 1979, i.e. 1 year after the shares would have been purchased for this exercise.

The average gain on these shares for the year was 41.8%. This is significantly better than the gain in the FT Index companies (17.3%) and the gain in the All Share Index (31.2%) during the same period of time. So, at least based on the prices for 1978, the potential profit is improved by selecting shares on the basis of their volatility rather than by just selecting a random from the whole market.

STRONG SHARES

The recent strength of a share is a second consideration in choosing our list of shares to buy. Since we are compiling our list of shares while the market is falling, so as to be ready to invest when the market recovers, it seems to be a reasonable assumption that shares which have not declined as much as the market in general, i.e. strong shares should be the ones in the forefront of the market recovery. In order to rank shares on this basis we need some method of quantifying the strength of a share. A way of doing this is to express the price of the share at the time when we have decided the market is definitely recovering as a percentage of its high value reached during the previous peak, i.e. in the present case its 1977/78 high value. Shares which have fallen from their previous peak, as we expect most of them to have done during the general decline, will have a price less than 100% of peak value. On the other hand, some shares may have moved ahead against the trend of the market during the period between when we tabulated the high–low values (i.e. during the early part of 1978) and when we are about to invest (i.e. 5th May 1978). These will give prices more than 100% of the previous peak, and can be considered to be the strongest shares as at 5th May. In Table 6.5 the results of this calculation are given under the heading 'Percentage of 1977/78 high'. By this means we can see that the strongest share was Automated Security with a price on 5th May 133.9% of its 1977/78 high (as the high stood in early 1978). The weakest share was Elliott Peterborough, where the price on 5th May (22p) was 50% of its 1977/78 high of 44p.

Table 6.5. Shares chosen in early 1978 on the basis of volatility: subsequent price movements

Share	1977/78 low	1977/78 high	Price 5 May 78	Percentage of 1977/78	Price at 4 May 79	Percentage gain (loss)
Breweries						
Arthur Bell	79	236	256	108.5	190 xd	(25.8)
Highland Distillers	52	158	143	90.5	102 xd	(28.7)
Whitbread	59	96½	99	102.6	147	48.5
					Average loss for sector	2.0%
Building						
Blue Circle	153	294	252	85.7	342 xd	35.7
Bryant	13	55	54	98.3	68 xd	25.8
John Carr	16½	48	46	95.8	65	41.3
Comben Group	13	38	31	81.6	40	29.0
Countryside	9	41	40	97.6	68	70.0
D. Crouch	22	99	87	87.9	128	47.1
Crouch Group	23	73	71	97.3	88	23.9
FPA Construction	7	26	23	88.5	13	(43.5)
Federated Land	13	47	46	97.9	79	71.7
Hoveringham	20	64	77 xd	120.3	96	24.7
Johnson-Richards	36	118½	130	109.7	166	27.7
London Brick	40	86	70	81.4	78	11.4
Marley	44	98	84	85.7	101	20.2
Monk	23½	86	100	116.3	170	70.0
Mowlem	44	143	124 xd	86.7	130	4.8
Newarthill	45	186	150 xd	80.6	270	80.0
Phoenix Timber	64	198	160	80.8	153	(4.4)
UBM	34	79	74½	94.3	76	2.0
					Average gain for sector	29.9%
Chemicals, Plastics						
Coalite	43½	78	77	98.7	83	6.5
Rentokil	34	62	58	93.5	118	103.4
Stewart Plastics	74	151	132	87.4	204	54.5
					Average gain for sector	54.8%
Stores						
Burton	50	142	126	88.7	347	175.4
Forminster*	30	91	102	12.1	168	64.7
Homecharm	60	122	148 xd	121.3	380	156.8
Lee Cooper	29½	137	135	98.5	302	123.7
Marks & Spencer	96	173	147	85.0	130	(11.6)
MFI	15½	76	78	102.6	380	387.2
Maple	5	17	19	111.8	31 xd	63.2
Ratners	17½	112	68	60.7	93	36.8
Austin Reed	32	98	86	87.8	147 xd	70.9
Rosgill	4	13½	14	103.7	31	121.4
Selincourt	10¾	28	26½	94.6	33	24.5
Shermans	3	11	12½	113.6	14½	16.0
Time Products	39	128	136	106.3	249	83.1
UDS	53	99	94	94.9	121	28.7
J. Walker	32	103	86	83.5	132	53.5
					Average gain for sector	93.0%
Electrical						
Automated Security	5½	59	79 xd	133.9	145 xd	83.5
Cableform	8¾	79	66	83.5	77	16.7

(Table continued)

Table 6.5. *(Continued)*

Share	1977/78 low	1977/78 high	Price 5 May 78	Percentage of 1977/78	Price at 4 May 79	Percentage gain (loss)
Comet Radiovision	29	115	122	106.1	162	32.7
Dubilier	9½	18½	17½	94.6	31½	80.0
Electrocomps.*	44	182½	199	109.0	312½	57.0
Energy Services	4½	14¼	11	77.2	30¼	170.5
EMI	141	254	144	56.7	114	(20.8)
Laurence Scott	44	136	123	90.4	94	(23.6)
Plessey	62	117	98	83.8	107	9.2
Pye Holdings	38	114	107	93.9	104	(2.8)
United Scientific	92	293	322	109.9	265	(17.7)
Wellco Holdings	9	27	25	92.6	36½	46.0

Average gain for sector 35.9%

Engineering

Babcock & Willcox	70	153	128	83.7	198 xd	54.7
Brooke Tool	11	28	32	114.3	48	50.0
John Brown	98	297	324	109.1	587	81.2
Bullough	65	142	125	88.0	270	116.0
Hawker Siddeley	113	214	214	100.0	266	24.3
Manganese Bronze	13	101	83	82.2	59	(28.9)
Metalrax	14	43	45	104.7	82	82.2
W. E. Norton	9	39	37	94.9	29	(21.6)
TACE	9½	51	29	56.9	31	6.9
Vickers	144	242	182	75.2	210	15.4

Average gain for sector 38.0%

Food

Barker & Dobson	3½	15	13¾	91.7	20	45.5
George Bassett	68	157	143	91.1	113	(21.0)
Hillards	89	300	195	65	300	53.8
Robertson	75	150	138	92	151	9.4

Average gain for sector 21.9%

Hotels

Grand Met	62	109	113	103.7	179	58.4
Ladbroke	89	215	201	93.5	220	9.5
Prince of Wales*	13	40	53	132.5	112	111.3

Average gain for sector 59.7%

Industrials

Associated Sprayers	14	35	33	94.3	68	106.0
Bath & Portland	28½	103	67	65.0	57	(14.9)
Beecham	372	693	664	95.8	725	9.2
Boots	115	244	219	89.8	235	7.3
Carlton Industries	57	175	185	105.7	275	48.6
Celestion	11½	37	35	94.6	35½	1.4
Centreway	54	210	242	115.2	360	48.8
Change Wares	5	35	24½	70.0	18	(26.5)
Cope Allman	37	65½	60½	92.4	80	32.2
Diploma	56	180	154	85.6	334	116.9
Dobson Park	37	79	83	105.1	117	41.0
Dundonian	24	64½	50	77.5	47	(6.0)
Duple	5½	14	14	100	27½	96.4
Eastern Produce	21	95	95	100	83	(12.6)
Elliott Peterboro	14	44	22	50	26	18.2
Elson & Robbins	37	79	101.3	100	26.6	

(Table continued)

Table 6.5. *(Continued)*

Share	1977/78 low	high	Price 5 May 78	Percentage of 1977/78	Price at 4 May 79	Percentage gain (loss)
George Ewer	15	27	28	103.7	41	46.4
Ferguson	37½	105	95	90.5	122	28.4
Fertleman	19	41	29	70.7	28	(3.4)
Gieves Group	30	96	101	106.2	134	32.7
Halma	14	64	60	93.8	68	13.3
Hunting Assoc.	74	218	220	100.9	233	5.9
Johnson Cleaners	27	86	100	116.3	152	52.0
Myson Group	38	74	73 xd	98.6	83 xd	13.7
Neil & Spencer	22	83	102	122.9	188	84.3
Parker Knoll	37	126	106	84.1	107	0.9
Pentland	6	26	21	80.8	34	61.9
Phillips Patents	6	19	15	78.9	23	53.3
Rank	128	276	248	89.9	286	15.3
Redfearn Glass	77	327	275	84.1	260	(5.5)
Reed Executive	15	47	52 xd	110.6	156	200.0
Securicor	46	87	98	112.6	188	91.8
Sketchley	55	109	102	93.6	186	82.4
Stag Furniture	28	114	102	89.5	197	93.1
Talbex	3	24½	23	93.9	13½	(41.3)
Toye	15	49	47	95.9	85	80.9
Turner & Newall	130	252	176	69.8	166 xd	(5.7)

Average gain for sector 39.3%

Leisure
Boosey & Hawkes	84	212	191	90.1	194 xd	1.6
Campari	25	132	131	99.2	121	(7.6)
Horizon	24	92	106 xd	115.0	260 xd	145.3
Zetters	21	55	55	100.0	74	34.5

Average gain for sector 12.9%

Shipping
Euro Ferries	53½	116	99	85.3	176	77.8
P & O	95	175	119½	68.3	86	(28.0)

Average gain for sector 24.9%

Textiles
J. Beales	33	67	55	82.1	67	21.8

Paper
Inveresk	46	83	66	79.5	49	(25.8)

Oils
Tricentrol	100	204	178	87.3	244	37.1

* Prices adjusted for splits and scrip issues.
xd = ex dividend

Since the overall objective of these exercises is to reduce the list of shares on the back pages of the *Financial Times* right down to a handful, say 30, then we can use this relative strength to reduce our list of the 118 most volatile shares. By doing this, we arrive at the 31 shares shown in Table 6.6. The reason for having 31 and not 30 shares is because the 30th place is shared by MFI and Whitbread. Since the gain for MFI was 387.2% and the gain for Whitbread was 48.5%, it would have been unfair to have left out either of these, which would have biased the results upwards or downwards. The leader, of course, in terms of relative strength at 5th May 1978 was Automated Security, whose price was nearly 34% higher than its price at its previous peak during 1977/8.

In order that we can justify the assertion that strength is a good criterion for selecting shares, we have to show that this group of 31 shares performed better than the 118 from which they were chosen. Table 6.6 lists the gains (or losses) which these shares made in the year from 5th May 1978, and we can see that the average gain was 76.3%. This has to be compared with the 41.8% gain which the 118 shares averaged for the year, which shows that

Table 6.6. The 31 strongest shares selected from the list of volatile shares given in Table 6.5. The shares are those which declined least or even advanced from their 1977/78 high values by 5th May 1978

Share	Price on 5 May 78 as percentage of 1977/78 high	Percentage gain (loss) in year to 4 May 79
Automated Security	133.9	83.5
Prince of Wales Hotels	132.5	111.3
Neil & Spencer	122.9	84.3
Homecharm	121.3	156.8
Hoveringham	120.3	24.7
Johnson Cleaners	116.3	52.0
Monk	116.3	70.0
Centreway	115.2	48.8
Horizon	115.2	145.3
Brooke Tool	114.3	50.0
Shermans	113.6	16.0
Securicor	112.6	91.8
Forminster	112.1	64.7
Maple	111.8	63.2
Reed Executive	110.6	200.0
United Scientific	109.9	(17.7)
Johnson Richards	109.7	27.7
John Brown	109.1	81.2
Electrocomponents	109.9	57.0
Arthur Bell	108.5	(25.8)
Time Products	106.3	83.1
Comet Radiovision	106.1	32.8
Carlton Industries	105.7	48.6
Gieves Group	105.2	32.7
Dobson Park	105.1	41.0
Metalrax	104.7	82.2
Rosgill	103.7	121.4
Grand Metropolitan	103.7	58.4
George Ewer	103.7	46.4
MFI	102.6	387.2
Whitbread	102.6	48.5

Average gain for group = 76.3%

picking shares on the basis of their recent strength was successful in improving our profit for the year. Only two shares, United Scientific and Arthur Bell, were standing lower at the end of the year. Thus in selecting a small number, say four to six shares from this list, there is only a small chance that one or even both of these losing shares would have been included.

On the question of the strength of shares, of course, one could take an opposite view to that put forward here. One might say that rather than select shares which have not declined very much during the fall of the market, we should select those shares which have fallen the furthest, since they have the greatest potential for profit when they recover. However, one has to ask why these shares have fallen further than the market. If there is no obvious reason, in terms of the company's profits, the loss of a large contract, some calamity at the factory, or political news which affects the company's prospects, etc., then perhaps the shares are oversold, and they may well undergo a dramatic reversal of the downward trend when the rest of the market recovers. What if, however, there is something fundamentally wrong with the company's prospects, or at least investors think there is something wrong? In that case, the trouble may not sort itself out, or be thought to be sorting itself out, in time for the market recovery, and the shares may continue their downward drift.

It is relatively easy to check on this contrary point of view by tabulating the gains or losses during the year for those 30 companies whose shares had declined the most during the market fall. These results are listed in Table 6.7, with the 'weakest' share being Elliot Peterborough, standing at 50% of the previous high, and the 30th share being Parker Knoll, standing att 84.1%. The overall gain in value in these shares at the end of the year was only 15.8%, which is much worse than the gain in the All Share Index, and very much worse than the performance of the 30 'strongest' shares, which showed a gain of 76.3% for the year. In addition to that, 11 of the 30 shares showed a loss for the period, and therefore the chance is very high that in a portfolio of say four or five shares, several of these losing shares would have been included.

Having reduced the thousands of shares in which it is possible to invest right down to the list of 31 shown in Table 6.6, we are not suggesting that the gain shown in the Table would have been made in practice. This is because we have not yet discussed selling techniques in this book. The following chapter on selling of shares will show that it is unlikely that any of the shares shown in Table 6.6, if bought on 5th May 1978 would still have been held a year later. Because of the 'fail-safe' mechanism built into the rules, the two losing shares, Arthur Bell and United Scientific, would actually have been sold at a profit because their price did move upwards from May 1978 onwards. It just happened that when they retreated from their peak they fell lower than their prices on 5th May 1978. The whole theme of this chapter is simply to develop a method of selecting shares such that they outperform the rest of the market over whichever time period we feel suitable to make a comparison. The time period has to be sufficiently long for the consistent nature of the improved performance to become obvious. Thus a 1-year period would appear to be satisfactory from this point of view, and showed convincingly that the two properties of high volatility and high relative strength at the moment a buying signal is given by the FT Index led to a vastly improved capital gain compared with a random selection of shares.

Of course it would be reckless to base an investment philosophy solely on an analysis of share price movements for 1 year. We have to adopt the same

Table 6.7. The 30 weakest shares selected from the list of volatile shares given in Table 6.5. The shares are those which declined the most from their 1977/78 high values by 5th May 1978.

Share	Price on 5 May 78 as percentage of 1977/78 high	Percentage gain (loss) in year to 4 May 79
Elliot Peterborough	50.0	18.2
EMI	56.7	(20.8)
TACE	56.9	6.9
Ratners	60.7	36.8
Hillards	65.0	53.8
Bath & Portland	65.0	(14.9)
P & O	68.3	(28.0)
Turner & Newall	69.8	(5.7)
Change Wares	70.0	(26.5)
Fertleman	70.7	(3.4)
Vickers	75.2	15.4
Energy Services	77.2	170.5
Dundonian	77.5	(6.0)
Phillips Patents	78.9	53.3
Guardian Royal	79.1	23.9
Inveresk	79.5	(25.8)
Alexanders	80.0	2.8
Zenith	80.0	(9.8)
Newarthill	80.6	80.0
Pentland	80.8	61.9
Phoenix	80.8	(4.4)
London Brick	81.4	11.4
Comben	81.6	29.0
J. Beales	82.1	21.8
Manganese Bronze	82.2	(28.9)
Cableform	83.5	16.7
J. Walker	83.5	53.5
Plessey	83.8	9.2
Babcock & Wilcox	83.7	54.7
Parker Knoll	84.1	0.9

Average gain for the group = 15.8%

Table 6.8. Shares chosen in April 1984 on the basis of the ratio of the high to low values: subsequent price movements

Share	1984 High	Low	Ratio	Price at 3 Aug. 84	Percentage of High 1984	Price at 11 May 85	Percentage gain or loss
Banks							
First Pacific	16	11	1.45	13	81.25	29	123.08
					Average gain for sector		123.08
Building							
Allied Plant	31	17	1.82	22	70.97	21.5	−2.27
Bailey (Ben)	45	27	1.67	33	73.33	24	−27.27
Condor Int	62	44	1.41	46	74.19	62	34.78
Helical Bar	77	20	3.85	24	31.17	28	16.67
Leech (Wm.)	102	70	1.46	115	112.75	174	51.30
Nott. Brick	133	72	1.85	110	82.71	145	31.82
Rowlinson Group	38	26	1.46	30	78.95	35	16.67
Ward Hldgs	144	63	2.29	132	91.67	170	28.79
					Average gain for sector		18.81%
Chemicals							
Canning (W.)	119	77	1.55	163	136.97	100	−38.65
Cory (Horace)	34	21	1.62	30.5	89.71	41	34.43
Croda Int.	138	92	1.50	120	86.96	135	12.50
Halstead J.	99	70	1.41	61	61.62	83	36.07
Yorks Chem.	68	38	1.79	43	63.24	65	51.16
					Average gain for sector		19.10%
Stores							
Allebone	43	24	1.79	39	90.70	52	33.33
Amber Day	44	11.5	3.83	9.5	21.59	10	5.26
Bolton Tex	26	18	1.44	19	73.08	20	5.26
Comb. Eng.	79	46	1.72	74	93.67	128	72.97
Ellis & Goldstein	61	34.5	1.77	54	88.52	80	48.15
Executex	48	28	1.71	28	58.33	28	.00
Grattan	104	66	1.58	90	86.54	208	131.11
Henriques	48	23	2.09	87	181.25	58	−33.33
Liberty	275	148	1.86	270	98.18	530	96.30
Lincroft	89	63	1.41	105	117.98	160	52.38
Sumrie	190	82	2.32	82	43.16	48	−41.46
Tern Consul	51	33	1.55	40	78.43	48	20.00
Woolworth	513	340	1.51	428	83.43	810	89.25
					Average gain for sector		36.86%
Electricals							
AB Electronic	555	366	1.52	408	73.51	440	7.84
Amstrad	124	80	1.55	72	58.06	84	16.67
Arcolectric	28	15	1.87	31	110.71	45	45.16
Arlen	170	55	3.09	47	27.65	53	12.77
Automated Sec	223	133	1.68	148	66.37	183	23.65
BSR	313	155	2.02	197	62.94	115	−41.62
Chloride	38	23	1.65	33	86.84	37	12.12
Crystallate	294	190	1.55	199	67.69	180	−9.55
CASE	199	104	1.91	205	103.02	278	35.61
Dataserve	110	68	1.62	77	70.00	134	74.03
Dewhurst	23.5	14	1.68	18	76.60	25	38.89
Fujitsu	431	217	1.99	402	93.27	370	−7.96
Molynx	46	24	1.92	27	58.70	56	107.41

(Table continued)

Table 6.8. *(Continued)*

Share	1984 High	Low	Ratio	Price at 3 Aug. 84	Percentage of High 1984	Price at 11 May 85	Percentage gain or loss
Multitone	155	90	1.72	86	55.48	65	−24.42
Rotaflex	118	64	1.84	114	96.61	154	35.09
Whitworth	78	50	1.56	58	74.36	65	12.07
					Average gain for sector		21.11%
Engineers							
Astra Ind.	19	10.5	1.81	14.5	76.32	6.75	−53.45
Banro	69	44	1.57	60	86.96	98	63.33
Birmid Qualcast	108	49	2.20	71.5	66.20	85	18.88
Blackwood Hodge	21	9	2.33	11.5	54.76	33	186.96
Brooke Tool	25.5	8	3.19	17	66.67	29	70.59
Brown J.	27	16	1.69	21	77.78	34	61.90
Camford Eng	39	18	2.17	23	58.97	35	52.17
Cronite Group	21	10	2.10	21.5	102.38	48	123.26
Dvs & Met.	98	65	1.51	47	47.96	62	31.91
Downiebrae	19	11	1.73	17	89.47	22	29.41
Elliott (B.)	60	36	1.67	43	71.67	81.5	89.53
Johnson & Firth	19	8	2.38	10.5	55.26	17	61.90
Manganese Bronze	50	33	1.52	57	114.00	66	15.79
Neepsend	18	9.5	1.89	13	72.22	16.5	26.92
Porter Chad	135	74	1.82	104	77.04	116	11.54
Renold	40	24	1.67	36.5	91.25	53	45.21
Richns. West	40	19.5	2.05	23	57.50	23	0.00
Senior Eng	32	16	2.00	17.5	54.69	25.5	45.71
Walker (C. & W.)	29	14.5	2.00	23	79.31	34	47.83
					Average gain for sector		48.92%
Food							
Bassett Foods	170	88	1.93	135	79.41	202	49.63
					Average gain for sector		49.63%
Hotels							
Ryan	11	7	1.57	14	127.27	26.5	89.29
					Average gain for sector		89.29%
Industrial							
Aberfoyle	42	14.5	2.90	31	73.81	38	22.58
Armour	38.5	24	1.60	21	54.55	20.5	−2.38
Ashley	28	13	2.15	14	50.00	21	50.00
Assoc. Br. Eng.	32	19	1.68	17	53.13	10	−41.18
Barget	48	30	1.60	18	37.50	*	
Bestwood	265	100	2.65	207	78.11	222	7.25
Booker McConnell	120	79	1.52	177	147.50	257	45.20
Brook St. Bur.	78	37	2.11	51	65.38	119	133.33
Burndene	20	9.5	2.11	13	65.00	20.5	57.69
Christie Tyler	48	31.5	1.52	41	85.42	43	4.88
Coins Inds.	115	75	1.53	52	45.22	42	−19.23
Comb. Tech.	33	17.5	1.89	16.5	50.00	26	57.58
Cosalt	80	43	1.86	69	86.25	62	−10.14
Diamond St.	48	24	2.00	31	64.58	30	−3.23
Emray	21.5	11.5	1.87	19.25	89.53	17	−11.69
Fobel	136	85	1.60	51	37.50	29	−43.14
Gestetner	109	60	1.82	60	55.05	103	71.67
Hyman (I. & J.)	36	17	2.12	21.5	59.72	32.5	51.16

(Table continued)

Table 6.8. *(Continued)*

Share	1984		Ratio	Price at 3 Aug. 84	Percentage of High 1984	Price at 11 May 85	Percentage gain or loss
	High	*Low*					
Jardine Math.	131	90	1.46	59	45.04	122	106.78
Kalamazoo	153	36	1.47	27	50.94	30	11.11
Kennedy Smale	148	78	1.90	120	81.08	100	−16.67
Lamont Hldgs	64	38	1.68	58	90.63	151	160.34
Newman Inds	33	16	2.06	17	51.52	35	105.88
Pollymark	19	12	1.58	14.5	76.32	10	−31.03
Prestwich Parker	78	36	2.17	65	83.33	147	126.15
Rockware	38	20	1.90	29	76.32	48	65.52
Rotaprint	14	10	1.40	6.5	46.43	6	−7.69
Solic. Law	40	26	1.54	26	65.00	36	38.46
Talbex	8.5	5.5	1.55	5.75	67.65	7.5	30.43
Triefus	63	33	1.91	41	65.08	39	−4.88
Waterford	45	21.5	2.09	27.5	61.11	47.5	72.73
Wolvhmtn St. Laund	43	24	1.79	17	39.53	38	123.53
					Average gain for sector		35.97%
Leisure							
Photax	66	35	1.89	46	69.70	43	−6.52
					Average gain for sector		−6.52%
Insurance							
Hogg Robinson	215	130	1.65	180	83.72	280	55.56
					Average gain for sector		55.56%
Motors							
Automotive	81	38	2.13	55	65.43	64	20.75
Alexanders	12	7	1.71	7.75	64.58	7.25	−6.45
Glanfield Lawr.	55	24	2.29	55	100.00	45	−18.18
					Average gain for sector		−1.29%
Shipping							
Lyle Shipping	112	77	1.45	32	28.57	10.5	−67.19
					Average gain for sector		−67.19%
Textiles							
Carpets Int.	69	37	1.86	23	33.33	69.5	202.17
Illingworth M.	40	19	2.11	34	85.00	84	147.06
Lowe (Robert H.)	49	23	2.13	26	53.06	26	0.00
					Average gain for sector		116.41%
Finance, Land							
Bonusbond	30	15	2.00	20	66.67	33	65.00
Oil							
Atlantic Res.	142	50	2.84	50	35.21	64	28.00
Bryson Oil Gas	470	205	2.29	383	81.49	147	−61.62
					Average gain for sector		−16.81%
Overseas traders							
African Lakes	63	28	2.25	47	74.60	88	87.23
Pat'son Zoch	152	90	1.69	113	74.34	165	46.02
Tozer Kems	44	26	1.69	31	70.45	38	22.58
					Average gain for sector		51.94%

attitude to the selection of shares as we did for determining buying profits. In the latter case we put forward the 13-week moving average because it had constantly been right in signalling substantial moves upward in the market for a considerable number of years. In the case of share selection, the procedure we have just worked through has also been consistently successful for a number of years in picking the winners. Since the most recent time period is the more relevant, and has the greatest impact, we can examine how the selection procedure has worked for 1984, taking the buying signal of 3rd August 1984 (see last chapter) as the starting point.

The most volatile shares, on the basis of the ratio of the high to low values for 1984 were chosen on 28th April 1984. These shares, 111 in all,

Table 6.9. The 30 'strongest' shares selected from the list of volatile shares given in Table 6.8. The shares are those which declined least or even advanced from their 1984 high values by 3rd August 1984

Share	Price on 3 Aug. 84 as percentage of 1984 high	Percentage gain (loss) in year to 11 May 85
Henriques	181.3	(33.3)
Booker McConnel	147.5	45.2
Canning (W.)	137.0	(38.6)
Ryan Hotels	127.2	89.2
Lincroft	117.9	52.3
Manganese Bronze	114.0	15.7
Leech Wm.	112.7	51.3
Arcolectric	110.7	45.1
CASE	103.0	35.6
Cronite	102.3	123.2
Glanfield Lawrence	100.0	(18.1)
Liberty	98.1	96.3
Rotaflex	96.6	35.0
Combined English Strs	93.6	72.9
Fujitsu	93.2	(7.9)
Ward Holdings	91.6	28.7
Renold	91.2	45.2
Allebone	90.7	33.3
Lamont	90.6	160.3
Cory (Horace)	89.7	34.4
Emray	89.5	(11.6)
Downiebrae	89.4	29.4
Ellis & Goldstein	88.5	48.1
Croda	86.9	12.5
Chloride	86.8	12.1
Grattan	86.5	131.1
Cosalt	86.2	(10.4)
Christie Tyler	85.4	4.8
Illingworth M.	85.0	147.0
Hogg Robinson	83.7	55.5
	Average gain for group	42.8%

are listed in Table 6.8. Their prices at 3rd August 1984, when the buying signal was given, are expressed as a percentage of the previous high value, so giving as before a means of deciding on the share strength. Also given in Table 6.8 are the prices on 11th May 1985, close to the time of writing, and the percentage gain or loss over the 9-month period. The average gain in the total number of 111 shares was 34.9%, whereas the FT 30 Index went from 831.4 to 1001.9, for a gain of 20.5% and the All Share Index from 499.14 to 632.33, a gain of 26.68% in the same period.

As in the previous case, it is instructive to select both the strongest 30 group from the list and the weakest 30, being judged in terms of their standing at 3rd August 1984 compared with the previous high on 28th April 1984. The strongest group is listed in Table 6.9, and run from Henriques, which

Table 6.10. The 30 'weakest' shares selected from the list in Table 6.8. The shares are those which declined the most from their 1984 high

Share	Price on 3 Aug. 84 as percentage of 1984 high	Percentage gain (loss) in year to 11 May 85
Amber Day	21.5	5.2
Arlen	27.6	12.7
Lyle Shipping	28.5	(67.1)
Helical Bar	31.1	16.6
Hyman J.	31.1	51.1
Carpets International	33.3	202.1
Atlantic Res.	35.2	28.0
Barget	37.5	(100.0)
Fobel	37.5	(43.0)
Wolverhampton St. Laundry	39.5	123.5
Sumrie	43.1	(41.6)
Jardine Mathieson	45.0	106.7
Coins Inds.	45.2	(19.3)
Rotaprint	46.4	(7.6)
Davies & Metcalfe	47.9	31.9
Ashley	50.0	50.0
Comb. Tech.	50.0	(10.1)
Kalamazoo	50.9	(11.1)
Newman	51.5	105.8
Lowe R.	53.0	0.0
Amour	54.5	(2.3)
Senior	54.6	45.7
Blackwood Hodge	54.7	186.9
Johnson & Firth	55.2	61.9
Multitone	55.4	(24.2)
Richs. West	57.5	0.0
Molynx	58.7	107.4
Camford Eng.	58.9	52.1
Hyman. I.	59.7	51.1

Average gain for group = 31.1%

Table 6.11. Summary of various gains made in 1978 and 1984 markets

Market	FT 30 Index	All Share Index	Volatile group	Strong group	Weak group
1978	17.3	31.2	41.8	76.3	15.8
1979	− 11.6	0.21	1.4	4.6	0.4
1984	20.5	26.6	34.9	42.8	31.1

stood at 181.3% of its 1984 high, down to Hogg Robinson, at 83.7% of its 1984 high. The average gain for the group by 11th May 1985 was 42.8%.

In Table 6.10 is shown those shares that were weakest on 3rd August 1984. These run from the weakest, Amber Day at 21.5% of its 1984 high, to Hyman (I. & J.) at 59.7% of its 1984 high. The average gain of this weaker group was 31.1%.

The first edition of this book also looked at the position of volatile shares during a market upturn in early 1979, and the current figures on the 1978 and 1984 markets plus this 1979 market are included in Table 6.11. The 1979 market is interesting because over the course of the following year to March 1980, the FT 30 Index actually fell back by over 11%, and the All Share Index virtually stood still. The table confirms fully that this method of selecting shares is able consistently to outperform the market in general. Indeed, even taking the volatile shares as a large group, rather than breaking them down into the 30 strongest shares, gives a performance that is very much better than either the FT 30 Index or the All Share Index.

For those investors with microcomputers the 'spreadsheet' type of program that is now available for virtually all microcomputers is ideal for the construction of the tables of shares, with automatic calculation of the ratios and percentage of the previous high value for each share. The table can be stored on disk and then retrieved and modified if necessary.

These share selections are now being carried out by means of a computer with a large storage facility, and are offered as a service to the private investor (see Appendix E).

Chapter 7

When to Sell

Correct selling is a much more difficult aspect of stock market investment than correct buying. The main reason for this is the greater number of psychological barriers which have to be overcome before carrying out a selling decision. In buying, usually the only problem is one of overcoming one's impatience to get invested, when frequently the wisest course is to wait a little longer until the appropriate signals appear to show that the investment climate has turned more favourable. In selling, the problems nearly all stem from the fact that you feel that you own a piece of the company and so form a kind of attachment to the shares of that company. It is much easier to do nothing than to take a positive decision to sell; selling appears to be an admission of failure, while holding on offers the prospect of being proved right in having bought the particular company's shares in the first place, if it recovers from what you are absolutely convinced is a temporary setback. A characteristic of nearly all amateur investors is an inability to accept that a share has passed its peak and to presume that the present hiccup in its upward trend is only one more of a number of temporary setbacks which it has suffered during its rise. After all, how are we to distinguish the present retreat from all the previous minor ones? By constantly convincing oneself that the turning point is just around the corner all the profit which accumulated from the correct decision to buy can be allowed to trickle, or even flood, away.

The reasonable way around this problem is twofold. Firstly, we must only treat company shares as pieces of paper, and form no other relationship with them other than that they are a means of making a profit. Secondly, we must have a rigid set of rules that tell us when to sell, and that must be obeyed instantly, without any ifs or buts. If sometimes they fail, that has to be accepted, but does not mean that we abandon the rules unless we can find better ones to put in their place. If our set of rules has worked reasonably well in the past at getting us out of a losing situation, we can reasonably expect them to do the same for us in the future. They will not work all the time, because nothing in the stock market can be predicted with absolute certainty, but if they work four times out of five we are bound to come out ahead in the long term, and that would be most unlikely if we based our selling decision upon personal feelings or instinct.

Our set of rules must err on the side of caution, since our overall philosophy is to increase our capital when market conditions are favourable, and preserve it from loss when conditions are unfavourable. It is far preferable to have sold and then see the shares continue on their upward path, than not to sell and then see them slide even further. If we have sold prematurely, we still have the option of repurchasing the same share, or of finding another one which we hope will rise, or even of depositing the money in a building society until the next change in market conditions. If we do end up buying the same shares again a few weeks later, we should look upon the commission we have paid on the 'round trip' as an insurance premium which we paid to protect our capital, and reflect that that happened to be the one case in five that the rules got us out too soon.

There are three useful methods that we can use to indicate when we should sell a particular holding. Two of these, which you will probably be most comfortable with until you gain experience, give unambiguous signals to sell, based simply upon numerical values which you have calculated. The third depends upon drawing trend lines (a fuller discussion appears in Chapter 8) and, therefore, is rather more subjective but with experience can be far superior to the numerical methods.

The first numerical method is based upon a 13-week moving average of the share price, while the second sets a floor which is the lowest price attained in the previous 9 months. A turndown of the average of a downwards penetration of the floor is the signal to sell.

THIRTEEN-WEEK MOVING AVERAGE

The method of calculating a moving average has been discussed already in Chapter 5. As pointed out there, a moving average gives us a line which is much smoother than the plot of the data from which it is derived. The gain in smoothness has to be paid for somehow, and this payment is the fact that the moving average is lagging in time behind the present. The value for a moving average always has to be plotted in the middle of the time span chosen, so that it is lagging behind by one-half of a time span. Thus, for a 13-week moving average, the value which has been computed from the last 13-weeks' closing prices must be plotted for the point 7 weeks back. Since our selling signal is based upon a turn-down in the moving average, then if we are computing this every week, this time lag makes no difference. As soon as this week's calculated value is less than last week's that is the signal to sell. Where this time lag does make a difference is when we are looking at graphs of the average plotted over a period of time, such as the examples in this chapter. In those cases, where we see on the graph that the average turned down on such and such a date, we must bear in mind that we would not have been aware at that time that it had turned down, until 7 weeks after that date. So, the price at which we would have sold would not be the price where it turned down on the chart, but the price exactly 7 weeks later.

To come back to the present, assuming a situation where we calculate each week the average for the last 13 weeks, then normally we would find that the share price has been falling for a few weeks before the average itself starts to fall. This few weeks of a fall is the penalty we have to pay for a greater degree of certainty that the upward trend in the share price has been reversed. Note that we do not mean 'absolute certainty', because nothing is absolutely certain in the stock market. We could increase our degree of certainty about the downturn in the trend of the share price by increasing the span of our moving average, say up to a 51-week moving average. When this turned down we could be even more sure that the rise in the share price was over. But, when you think about it, the delay in that average would be 26 weeks, i.e. 26 weeks would have elapsed before we got a selling signal, by which time of course the share price could have gone down to the basement.

The 13-week moving average is a reasonable compromise between certainty that the share price has started to move down, and receiving a selling signal soon enough to get out before the price has retreated too far from its peak. On past performance, in the case of the vast majority of share prices, a turndown in the 13-week moving average has nearly always signalled a prolonged fall in the share price lasting for a few months. The 13-week moving average has also been fairly successful in not giving selling signals when the dip in the share price is only of a temporary nature, i.e. usually it does not shake us out of a share unnecessarily.

To see how successful this method is, we can look at the weekly closing prices and 13-week moving averages for Babcock, which are plotted in Figs 7.1(a) and 7.1(b). Figure 7.1(a) is identical to the one published in the first edition of this book, but as discussed in the Appendix, because microcomputers are now commonplace, and are extremely useful for carrying out such operations as the calculation of moving averages, they can be used to produce charts such as the one in Figure 7.1(b). This latter chart, in two parts, covers the period from the beginning of 1980 to the present, and the 13-week moving average in this case is the heavier smooth line superimposed upon the price data.

Because of the time lag, the moving average terminates 7 weeks before the end of the weekly data. The arrows give the points at which the average

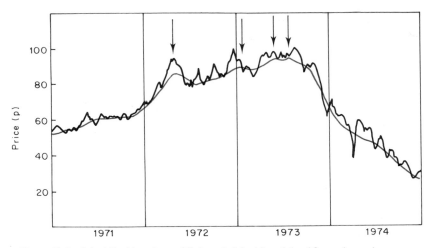

Figure 7.1. (a). Weekly prices of Babcock (black) and the 13-week moving average (red) from 1971 to 1974,

can be seen to have started to turn downwards. Table 7.1 shows the share prices current at the time the average turned down (7 weeks on from the arrows), along with the peaks attained several weeks before the average gave a 'sell' signal. This then gives us an idea of how much profit has been lost from the peak of the share price, which in turn gives us an indication as to how efficient the signal has been in protecting most of our profit. That the selling signal generated by this method is a very useful one can be judged by the fact that the 18 selling signals got us out at an average value of 12.5% below the peak price at that period of time. There is no way that selling by instinct can maintain that kind of consistency over a number of selling operations, and most investors would be quite happy to settle for a method which brings them out within about 12% of the top.

On their own these selling points do not tell us much about the profit we would have made unless we have also established our buying points. So, although there are four selling signals throughout the period 1972 and 1973, our buying signals, based on the 13-week average of the FT Index, would not have allowed us to buy again during this period after the selling signal of 16th June 1972. By following the buying principle outlined in Chapter 5, we would have bought Babcock in early 1971 at a price of about 55p, and our selling signal would have got us out in June 1972 at 79p, for a gain of 43.6% over the period. The market next signalled a purchase on 24th January 1975. Babcock shares could then have been bought for 28p. At the selling signal on 18th July we would have obtained 60p for them, a gain of 114.3%. The next buying signal was on 19th September 1975, at which time Babcock shares were 77p and we would have sold again on 16th July 1976

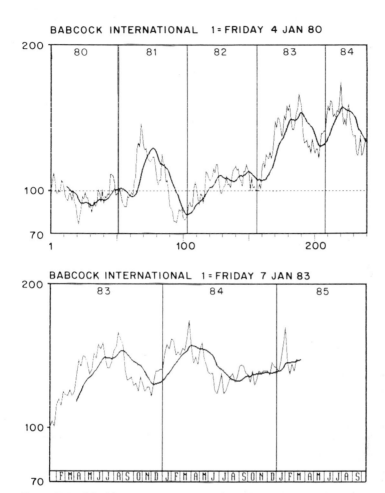

BABCOCK INTERNATIONAL   1 = FRIDAY 4 JAN 80

BABCOCK INTERNATIONAL   1 = FRIDAY 7 JAN 83

Figure 7.1. (b). Microcomputer plot of weekly prices of Babcock shares and the 13-week moving average from (i) 1980 to mid-1984 (ii) 1983 to May 1985.

at 84p, a gain of 9.1%. The FT 13-week average next indicated a buying situation on 31st December 1976, when Babcock were 61p and the next selling signal got us out on 4th November 1977, at 106p for a gain of 73.8%. A buying signal came again on 12th May 1978 when Babcock were 123p and they would have been sold again at the end of December 1978 for 147p, i.e. a gain of 19.5%. The next buying signal came on 9th March 1979, when Babcock could have been bought for a price of 169p and a selling price came on 15th June 1979 at a price of 155p for a loss of 8.3%. A small gain of 3.4% would have been made by buying on 13th June 1980 and selling on 11th July of that year. A buying signal came on 27th February 1981 when

Table 7.1. Selling signals in Babcock, based on the 13-week moving average

Date turn-down in average became apparent	Share price (p)	Date share price peaked out	Peak price	Percentage below peak when signalled
16 June 72	79	18 Apr. 72	94	16.0
2 Mar. 73	83	15 Dec. 82	100	17.0
11 July 73	94	1 June 73	98	4.1
14 Sept. 73	93	17 Aug. 73	101	7.9
18 July 75	60	7 June 75	69	13.0
16 July 76	84	22 May 76	89	5.6
4 Nov. 77	106	9 Sept. 77	140	24.3
29 Dec. 78	147	28 Oct. 78	166	11.4
15 June 79	155	4 May 79	198	21.7
11 July 80	95	20 June 80	96	1.0
26 Sept. 80	92	12 Sept. 80	101	8.9
12 Dec. 80	97	21 Nov. 80	111	12.6
3 July 81	123	24 Apr. 81	146	15.7
2 July 82	101	4 June 82	118	14.4
26 Nov. 82	100	5 Nov. 82	118	18.0
15 July 83	141	24 June 83	159	11.3
13 Apr. 84	149	23 Mar. 84	174	14.3
5 Oct. 84	132	7 Sept. 84	144	8.3
			Average =	12.5%

Babcock were 97p, and was followed by a selling signal on 3rd July 1981 when they were 123p, for a gain of 26.8%, while later in 1981, on 18th December, a buying signal saw Babcock at 81p. The corresponding selling signal came on 2nd July 1982 when they were 101p, for a gain of 24.7%. Only one buying opportunity occurred in 1982, on 24th September at 115p, and the selling signal on 26th November of that year at 100p resulted in a loss of 13.0%. It was another year until the next buying opportunity on 25th November 1983 at 121p with a selling signal on 6th April 1984 at 145p for a gain of 19.8%. Finally to the time of writing there was a buying signal on 31st August 1984 at 142p which resulted in a loss of 7.0% when the selling signal came at 132p on 5th October 1984. These buying and selling operations are summarized in Table 7.2.

It is an interesting point that of the 12 selling signals generated by the 13-week moving average, no less than five of them occurred in a July.

If the proceeds of selling were reinvested in the next buying operation, the cumulative gain over the five 'round trip' transactions from 1971 to 1984 would have been 913%, so that the capital value would have increased by a factor of about ten in a period of 13 years. The average gain per investment was 25.5%, and a study of the dates in Table 7.2 shows that the average period of investment was about 6 to 7 months. This therefore represents a good rate of return, even allowing for the commissions involved in buying and selling, which have not been taken into account.

Table 7.2. Buying and selling operations in Babcock shares as signalled by 13-week moving averages (FT Index for buying and share price for selling)

Buying		Selling		
Date	Share price (p)	Date	Share price (p)	Percentage gain (loss)
20 Feb. 71	55	16 June 72	79	43.6
24 Jan. 75	28	18 July 75	60	114.3
19 Sept. 75	77	16 July 76	84	9.1
31 Dec. 76	61	4 Nov. 77	106	73.8
12 May 78	123	29 Dec. 78	147	19.5
9 Mar. 79	169	15 June 79	155	(8.3)
13 June 80	88	11 July 80	91	3.4
27 Feb. 81	97	3 July 81	123	26.8
18 Dec. 81	81	2 July 82	101	24.7
24 Sept. 82	115	26 Nov. 82	100	(13.0)
25 Nov. 83	121	6 Apr. 84	145	19.8
31 Aug. 84	142	5 Oct. 84	132	(7.0)

Average gain per investment = 25.5%
Cumulative gain = 913%

A vast number of examples could be given here on the operation of the 13-week moving average as a selling signal. However, it is suggested that you carry out such calculations on a share or shares which you have chosen by the method outlined in the last chapter. The data for the shares for a large number of companies for several years back can be obtained either from share price charts or from printed data sheets which are sometimes available. These are as mentioned in Appendix E.

The turn-down in the 13-week moving average has been useful in develop-

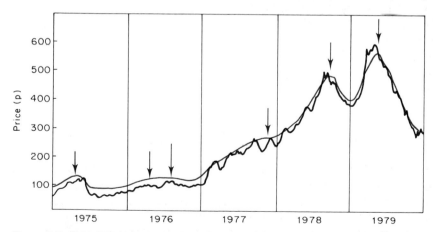

Figure 7.2. (a). Weekly prices of John Brown (black) and the 13-week moving average (red) from 1975 to 1979. Arrows show the selling signals.

ing selling signals for all shares, but is not always as successful in getting us out as near to the peak price as the Babcock case. One example in which this method was less successful is John Brown. A plot of the weekly closing prices and the 13-week average for John Brown shares is shown in Fig. 7.2(a). Once again, arrows show the points at which selling signals were generated. The dates, 7 weeks after the position of the arrows, at which a turn-down in the average became apparent were: 7th June 1975, 28th May 1976, 1st October 1976, 16th December 1977, 4th November 1978 and 15th June 1979. As in the case of Babcock shares, charts of John Brown shares since 1980, together with the 13-week moving averages produced by

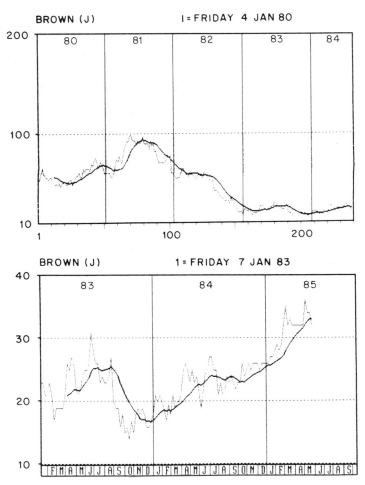

Figure 7.2. (b). Microcomputer plot of weekly prices of John Brown shares and the 13-week moving average from (i) 1980 to mid-1984; (ii) 1983 to May 1985.

microcomputer, are also shown in Figure 7.2(b). In this case selling signals were generated on 19th December 1980, 17th July 1981, 30th April 1982, 15 July 1983, 24th February 1984 and 13th July 1984.

Table 7.3 shows these 12 signals based on the 13-week moving averages, the share prices at the time the signals were given and the dates and prices of the peak values attained by the shares prior to the selling signals. In this case, for the 12 selling signals, we would have sold at prices averaging 15.0% down from the peak prices at those times. Thus, this is an inferior performance of the selling signals compared with Babcock.

As in the case of Babcock, it is important to look at a complete picture of buying and selling operations. Of the selling signals listed in Table 7.3, the one on 1st October 1976 is superfluous, since the rules we have established for buying would not have allowed us to buy again following the sale on 28th May 1976, until 30th December 1976. A similar comment applies to the signals of 18th December 1981 and 24th September 1982. During the period in question it would have been possible to carry out nine complete buying and selling operations. These are summarized in Table 7.4. The most successful 'round trip' was the purchase on 30th December 1976 at 97p, which led to a sale on 16th December 1977 at 250p, for a gain of 157.7%. By reinvesting the proceeds of each sale into the next buying operation, a cumulative gain of 712% would have been obtained over the nine transactions between 24th January 1975 and 14th September 1984, i.e. over a period of only just over 9 years! The average gain per investment would have been 32.5%. This gain has, of course to be compared with the time period for which one is invested. This works out as about 5 to 6 months,

Table 7.3. Selling signals in John Brown shares, based on the 13-week moving average

Date turn-down in average became apparent	Share price	Date share peaked out	Peak price	Percentage below peak when signalled
7 June 75	75	24 May 75	115	34.8
28 May 76	82	21 May 76	90	8.9
1 Oct. 76	90	14 Aug. 76	105	14.3
16 Dec. 77	250	2 Dec. 77	260	3.8
4 Nov. 78	415	13 Sept. 78	490	15.3
15 June 79	494	4 May 79	587	15.8
19 Dec. 80	59	31 Oct. 80	77	27.1
17 July 81	90	10 July 81	97	7.2
30 Apr. 82	57	19 Mar. 81	61	6.5
15 July 83	23	17 June 83	31	25.0
24 Feb. 84	18	20 Jan. 84	21	14.2
13 July 84	25	6 July 84	27	7.4
				Average = 15.0%

Table 7.4. Buying and selling operations in the shares of John Brown, as signalled by 13-week moving averages

Buying		Selling		
Date	Share price (p)	Date	share price (p)	Percentage gain
24 Jan. 75	70	7 June 75	75	7.1
19 Sept. 75	52	28 May 76	82	57.7
31 Dec. 76	97	16 Dec. 77	250	157.7
5 May 78	310	4 Nov. 78	415	33.9
9 Mar. 79	478	15 June 79	494	3.3
13 June 80	51	12 Dec. 80	59	15.6
27 Feb. 81	73	17 July 81	90	23.2
25 Nov. 83	19	24 Feb. 84	18	(5.2)
31 Aug. 84	23	14 Sept. 84	23	0.0

Average gain per investment = 32.5%
Cumulative gain = 712%

as can be seen from the dates in Table 7.4. By any standards this is quite a good return, even allowing for the inevitable buying and selling costs. The reader should by now be convinced that this method of moving averages has great merit as a means of protecting the greater proportion of the gains which your share has accumulated since the buying signal.

BREAKING THE 9-WEEK LOW

This method consists of superimposing upon a plot of the share price the lowest level attained in the previous 9 weeks, but excluding the current week's data. In the case of a rising share price, this 9-week low moves up from time to time under it. If the share price drops to a point which penetrates this low, this is taken as a signal to sell. There is a similar problem here in choosing the period for which the low operates, i.e. 9 weeks in our case, as there was in the case of a moving average. Too short a low period, such as 3 or 4 weeks, could mean that the sale is triggered when the price undergoes only a very temporary setback. Too long a period means that the price has to fall a long way before a selling signal is given. This would mean too large a loss to be acceptable. Because of these factors, calculations on a large number of share prices have shown that a 9-week low is an ideal compromise.

In order to keep a valid comparison with the 13-week moving average method, we shall apply the 9-week low method to the same share prices, Babcock and John Brown. In Fig. 7.3(a) are plotted the weekly closing prices and the 9-week lows for Babcock for 1971 to 1979. As can be seen from the number of arrows marking the points where the 9-week low was penetrated, this method gives more signals than the moving average: 11 points as opposed to eight. There is no problem of a time lag in the case of violation of the 9-week low, the dates shown on the plot being the dates at which we knew the low was broken and, therefore, the date at which we would have sold the shares. The selling points were 2nd June 1972, 2nd March 1973, 14th September 1973, 14th June 1974, 18th July 1975, 6th August 1976, 29th July 1977, 4th November 1977, 24th February 1978, 9th February 1979 and 15th June 1979. As with the moving averages, calculating and plotting the 9-week low is an ideal task for a microcomputer, and such a plot is presented in Figure 7.3(b) for the period to early 1985. The selling points and appropriate share prices for both the 9-week low method and the 13-week moving average method are given in Table 7.5.

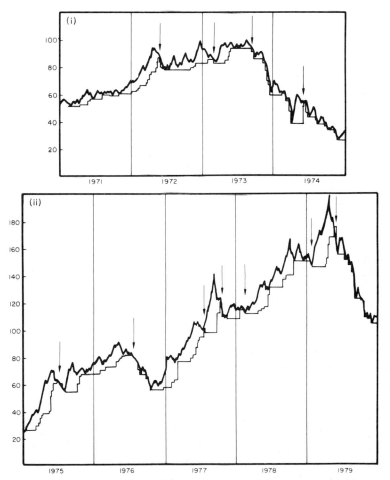

Figure 7.3. (a). Weekly prices of Babcock (heavy line) and the 9-week low (light line) (i) from 1971 to 1974; (ii) 1975 to 1979. Arrows show the selling signals.

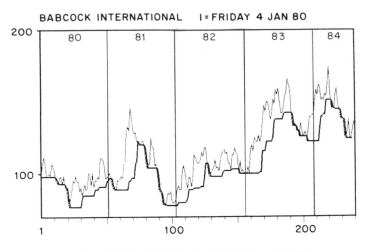

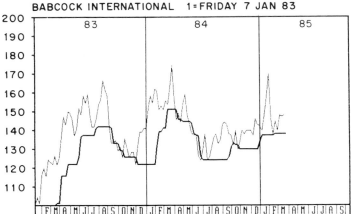

Figure 7.3. (b). Microcomputer plot of weekly prices of Babcock shares and the 9-week low (heavy line) (i) from 1980 to mid-1984; (ii) 1983 to May 1985.

The first selling signal, on 2nd June 1972, came 2 weeks before the appropriate moving average signal, enabling us to sell at 81 as opposed to 79. The next three signals are irrelevant because, as shown earlier in Table 7.2, we would not have reinvested until 24th January 1975. The next selling on 18th July 1975 was identical for both methods. We would have reinvested again on 19th September 1975 and the next selling came on 6th August 1976. This is later by 3 weeks and worse by 7p a share than the signal given by the moving average. We would have reinvested on 31st December 1976 and the 9-week low method would have got us out on 29th July 1977 at 96p, at a period when the moving average gave no signal. Both methods signalled a sale on 4th November 1977 at 106p. We would have bought again on 12th May 1978 and sold on 9th February 1979 at 143p, according to the 9-week

Table 7.5. A comparison of the selling points and share prices of the 9-week low and 13-week moving average methods for Babcock shares since 1971

Buying		13-week average		9-week low	
Date	Share price (p)	Date	Price (p)	Date	Price (p)
20 Feb. 71	55	16 June 72	79	2 June 82	81
24 Jan. 75	28	18 July 75	60	18 July 75	60
19 Sept. 75	77	16 July 76	84	6 Aug. 76	77
1 Dec. 76	61	4 Nov. 77	106	29 July 77	96
12 May 78	123	29 Dec. 78	147	9 Feb. 79	143
9 Mar. 79	169	15 June 79	155	15 June 79	155
13 June 80	88	11 July 80	91	17 Jan. 81	92
27 Feb. 81	97	3 July 82	123	5 June 81	121
18 Dec. 81	81	2 July 82	101	18 June 82	100
24 Sept. 82	115	26 Nov. 82	100	26 Nov. 82	100
25 Nov. 83	121	6 Apr. 84	145	24 Apr. 84	144
31 Aug. 84	142	5 Oct. 84	132	5 Oct. 84	132

low method. However, by comparison, the moving average method would have told us to sell 2 months earlier, on 29th December 1978 at 147p. We would have bought again on 9th March 1979 and the 9-week low method would have told us to sell on 15th June 1979 at 155p, the same week as the 13-week average signalled. Buying again on 15th June 1980, the moving average method would have got us out on 11th July of the same year, whereas the 9-week low method would have left us in until 4th January 1981, gaining an extra 1p per share in the process. The next buying opportunity came on 27th February 1981, the moving average taking us out on 3rd July 1981 at 123p. The 9-week low would have had us selling a month earlier at 121p on 5th June. We would have bought again on 18th December 1981 and again the 9-week low would have taken us out earlier, on 18th June 1982 at 100p compared with 2nd July 1982 at 101p. After buying on

Table 7.6. Comparison of selling point and share prices of the 13-week average and 9-week low method for John Brown shares since 1975

Buying		13-week average		9-week low	
Date	Share price (p)	Date	Price (p)	Date	Price (p)
24 Jan. 75	70	7 June 75	75	7 June 75	75
19 Sept. 75	52	28 May 76	82	4 June 76	75
31 Dec. 76	97	16 Dec. 77	250	8 Apr. 77	145
5 May 78	310	4 Nov. 78	415	28 Oct. 78	425
9 Mar. 79	478	15 June 79	494	25 May 79	525
13 June 80	51	12 Dec. 80	59	12 Dec. 80	59
27 Feb. 81	73	17 July 81	90	24 July 81	89
25 Nov. 83	19	24 Feb. 84	18	1 June 84	19
31 Aug. 84	23	14 Sept. 84	23	31 May 85	31

24th September 1982, both methods would have given a selling signal on the same date, 26th November 1982 at 100p. A year later on 25 November 1983 it was time to buy again, and this time the moving average signal came first, on 6th April 1984 at 145p compared with the 9-week low on 24th April at 144p. The last buying opportunity by the time of writing was on 31st August 1984, and both methods generated selling signals on the same day, 5th October 1984 at 132p.

The final results obtained by either of these methods can be seen, from Table 7.5, to be fairly similar in the case of Babcock shares.

As far as John Brown is concerned, more signals were given by the 9-week low method, as can be seen from the plot of the weekly closing prices and the 9-week low for the period since 1975, in Figs 7.4(a) and (b).

As a comparison with the 13-week average method, the selling points and prices for both the methods for John Brown shares for the period 1975 to 1979 are given in Table 7.6.

There is rather more divergence between the two methods in the case of John Brown shares than there was with Babcock shares. The 9-week low method got us out far too early after the buying opportunity on 31st December 1976, but on the other hand was superior in both the March 1979 and August 1984 markets.

For a wide range of shares the 9-week low method signals a selling situation a week or so before the moving average on about three occasions out of five; for the other two the moving average comes first. On the other hand, the 9-week low method also gives us some false signals that cause us to sell prematurely. A premature sale should not cause us to shed any tears for lost profits, however, since we can live to fight another day; probably the best approach to these two methods is to follow both of them, and act

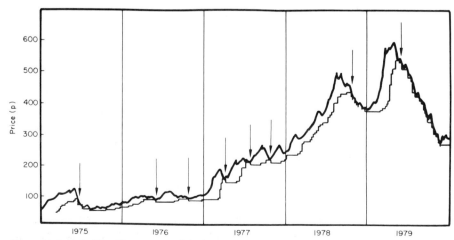

Figure 7.4. (a). Weekly prices of John Brown (heavy line) and the 9-week low (light line) from 1975 to 1979. Arrows show the selling signals.

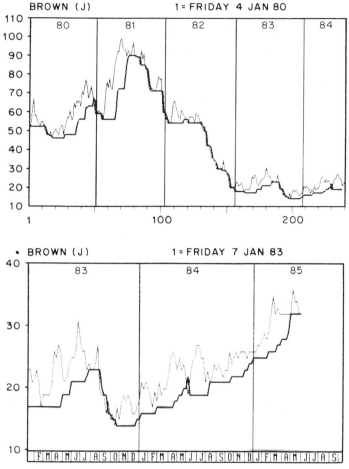

Figure 7.4. (b). Microcomputer plot of weekly prices of John Brown shares and the 9-week low (heavy line), (i) from 1980 to mid-1984; (ii) 1983 to May 1985.

on whichever signal comes first. If they both appear at the same time, so much the better. On those occasions when the 9-week low signals first, it is possible to gain some confirmation by checking the 13-week average to see if there are any signs of it slowing down in its rate of increase, which it should do a week or so before it actually turns down.

THE RISE–FALL TRENDLINE

When a share price rises over a period of many weeks, a close look at the weekly closing prices during that time usually shows that the price does not rise consistently, week after week, but advances for a few weeks, then slips

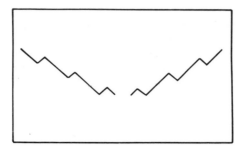

Figure 7.5. Idealized versions of the way in which share prices rise and fall over short periods of time.

back perhaps for a week before advancing further. This may happen several times during the course of its rise, so we have a sort of 'two steps forward, one step back' type of situation. The rising price is the result of two things: firstly, the price increase during the weeks the price goes up is greater than the price fall during the weeks it falls, and secondly, the number of weeks for which it advances is greater than the number during which it declines. This is not an invariable fact, but does appear to be true for the majority of occasions. When a share price is falling over a period of many weeks the opposite will be true—during the period the weekly price falls are greater than the weekly price rises, and the number of weeks for which the price falls is greater than the number of weeks during which the price rises. Idealized versions of both of these situations are shown in Fig. 7.5.

The previous two numerical methods for generating selling signals utilized the changes in the share prices themselves as the basis of the methods, and the number of advancing weeks relative to the number of declining weeks during the overall period of advance of the share price was not of particular importance. The third method for generating selling signals, however, concentrates on this latter aspect and neglects the actual

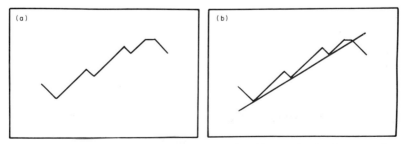

Figure 7.6. (a) The rise–fall indicator plotted for the shares whose prices are given in Table 7.7. (b) a trend line drawn on the rise–fall indicator from (a).

prices themselves. The indicator assumes that a rising price tends to follow a pattern of x weeks upwards and y weeks downward (where x and y are quite small, say 3 or 4 to 1 or 2 respectively), the pattern being repeated

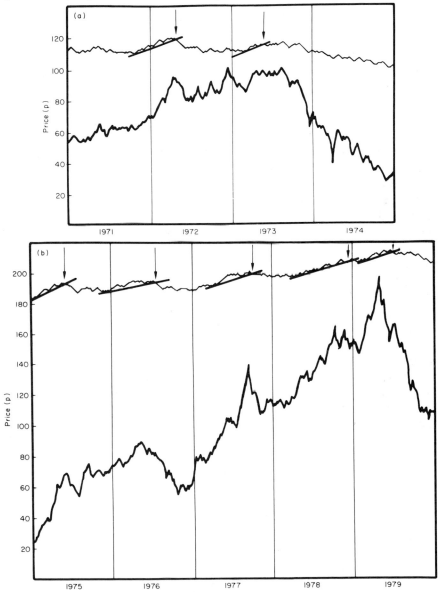

Figure 7.7. Weekly closing prices of Babcock (heavy line) and the rise–fall indicator (light line) (a) from 1971 to 1974, (b) from 1975 to 1979. Selling points are indicated by arrows at the points where the trend lines (short heavy lines) are penetrated by the rise–fall indicator.

several times. It is the break in this pattern which is considered to signal an impending down-turn to the actual share price, so therefore tells us to sell.

The indicator itself is extremely easy to plot. At the beginning of the time period we are interested in, we set it at an arbitrary value, such as zero, and each week we increase it by one every time a price is higher than the previous week, and decrease it by one if the price is lower. If the price is unchanged we give the indicator the same value as last week. A weekly record of such an indicator for some mythical share prices is given in Table 7.7.

We can then plot this indicator on the same graph as the share price itself, using the same weeks for the values, but a different vertical scale for the indicator, since it moves only one point (or zero) at a time, whereas the share price of course may move perhaps by 50p a week (Fig. 7.6(a)). The indicator does not itself give us a selling signal. To obtain such a signal it is necessary to draw a trend line. This is done by joining the bottom points of the saw-tooth shape in Fig. 7.6(a) by a straight line. It will be unlikely that we can join more than two or three such points following a change in direction of the saw-tooth from down to up. Having then established this trend line, our selling signal is given when the indicator, instead of bouncing back up from this line, penetrates it downwards (Fig. 7.6(b)).

Applied to a real case, we can see this indicator, and the weekly closing prices plotted for Babcock shares from 1971 to 1979, in Figs 7.7(a) and (b). There are seven trend lines drawn for those situations where the share price is obviously rising: in 1972, 1973, 1975, 1976, 1976/77, 1978 and 1979. For each trend line the rise–fall indicator approached it several times and bounced back before finally penetrating it. So, when the indicator turns down towards the trend line we have to watch carefully for that time when it does not bounce back, that being then our selling signal. The dates at which this happened, and corresponding share prices, are given in Table 7.8.

A comparison of Table 7.8 with Table 7.5 shows that this indicator was superior to both the 13-week moving average method and the 9-week low

Table 7.7. Construction of a weekly rise–fall indicator

Week	Share price	Indicator	Week	Share price	Indicator
1	222	0	10	245	3
2	220	− 1	11	250	4
3	210	− 2	12	260	5
4	215	− 1	13	255	4
5	220	0	14	260	5
6	225	1	15	270	6
7	230	2	16	270	6
8	225	1	17	265	5
9	235	2	18	260	4

Table 7.8 Selling signals for Babcock shares as given by the penetration of trend lines by the rise–fall indicator

Date	Price	Date	Price
11 May 72	90	7 Oct. 77	120
1 June 73	95	29 Dec. 78	147
21 June 75	68	8 June 79	177
28 May 76	81		

method. Except for the May 1976 signal, the other signals gave selling indications when the share price was much higher than with the other two methods. Except for 29th December 1978 the signals also came much sooner—several weeks—than the signals from the numerical methods.

The best way of showing the superiority of the rise–fall method over the other two is to calculate the overall gain which would have been achieved by using it in transactions in Babcock. The gains for the buying and selling operations which fell between 1971 and 1979 are shown in Table 7.9. The overall gain for the period was 928%. For the corresponding period using the 13-week average as a selling indicator, the overall gain would have been 539%. Therefore, assuming reinvestment of proceeds from sales, by using the rise–fall indicator, the capital value would have been increased by a factor of more than ten during the period.

Having shown that this indicator was far superior in giving selling signals for Babcock, it remains to show whether it was superior in the case of John Brown shares, since the chart pattern for this share was rather different from that of Babcock. This indicator and the share prices for John Brown, between 1975 and 1979 are shown in Fig. 7.8. In the period from 1975 to 1979 there are five trend lines which were penetrated on 3rd May 1975, 6th February 1976, 5th August 1977, 29th September 1978 and 6th April 1979.

Table 7.9. Buying and selling operations in Babcock shares between 1971 and 1979, as signalled by the 13-week moving average of the FT Index for buying and the rise–fall indicator for selling

Buying		Selling		
Date	Price	Date	Price	Percentage gain
20 Feb. 71	55	11 May 72	90	63.6
24 Jan. 75	28	21 June 75	68	142.9
19 Sept. 75	77	28 May 76	81	5.2
31 Dec. 76	61	7 Oct. 77	120	96.7
12 May 78	123	30 Dec. 78	147	19.5
9 Mar. 79	169	8 June 79	177	4.7
		Cumulative gain = 928%		

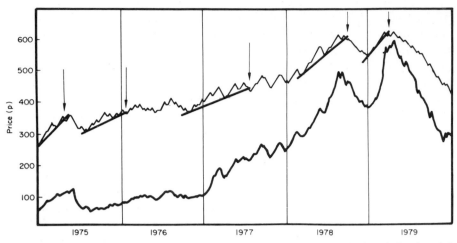

Figure 7.8. Weekly closing prices of John Brown shares (heavy line) and the rise—fall indicator (light line) from 1974 to 1979. Selling points are indicated by arrows at the points where the trend lines are penetrated by the rise—fall indicator.

The buying and selling operations carried out on John Brown shares, using the 13-week moving average of the FT Index for buying, and the breaking of the trend lines by the rise—fall indicator for selling, are given in Table 7.10.

The cumulative gain on five transactions in John Brown shares, using the rise—fall indicator as a selling indicator, is 575%, i.e. the starting capital would have increased by a factor of nearly seven times by this method over the period 1975 to 1979. This is a gain of nearly 90% more than would have been achieved using the 13-week moving average signal for selling.

In these two cases, of Babcock and John Brown shares, the breaking of the trend line of the rise—fall indicator has given a far better signal for

Table 7.10. Buying and selling operations in John Brown shares between 1975 and 1979, as signalled by the 13-week moving average of the FT Index for buying and the rise—fall indicator for selling

Buying		Selling		
Date	*Price*	*Date*	*Price*	*Percentage gain*
24 Jan. 75	70	3 May 75	95	35.7
19 Sept. 75	52	6 Feb. 76	75	44.2
31 Dec. 76	97	5 Aug. 77	210	116.5
12 May 78	310	29 Sept. 78	435	40.3
9 Mar. 79	478	6 Apr. 79	543	13.6
			Cumulative gain	= 575%

selling of the three methods we have discussed. Again this is true for a wide range of shares but there is the slight disadvantage that it takes rather more experience to draw the trend line correctly than is the case with the other methods, which depend upon simple numerical calculation. A more major disadvantage is that it is difficult to program a microcomputer to carry out the task. The construction of the rise–fall indicator by computer is of course straightforward, but the difficulty comes with the drawing of the trend lines which, as we have seen, is not an objective exercise. The rise–fall indicator method is therefore best for those investors who have a reasonable amount of time at their disposal.

It is suggested that you do not plunge immediately into this trend line signal, but again experience by applying it to a large number of share prices, obtained from charts as mentioned before. When you are quite happy about your ability to use it you can then consider it to be your major indicator for selling, and use it with confidence. As shown in the above examples, this indicator usually gives its signal some weeks before the moving average or 9-week low methods, and so, when the trend line gives a signal, some slight confirmation should be forthcoming from the other methods in the form of a reduction of share price downwards towards its 9-week low floor.

Although we have shown so far how these selling signals have performed in the case of two shares over a number of years, it might still be argued that the examples are too few to really prove the point about selling signals, and that we need to show many more such examples to be really convincing. In the last chapter we chose a list of 31 shares, on the basis of volatility and relative strength. We showed that during the year following the buying signal in May 1978, our 'top 31' outperformed both the market in general and the Financial Times 30 shares in particular, in terms of percentage gain for the group. In one sense the selection was perhaps not too meaningful, because we made the assumption that the shares were held for a whole year when we calculated the percentage gain. This ignored any selling signals that might have been generated during the year and gave the results which we showed in Table 6.5. However, if we look at what would have been real-life situations, in which we kept track of the 13-week moving average, the 9-week low, and the rise–fall indicator, then we would have achieved the gains and losses shown in Table 7.11. This table gives, for each of the 'top 31' shares which were listed in Table 6.5, the times the selling signals were given, and the relevant prices. Now we have a much wider basis on which to compare the relative merits of the three different types of selling signal. The table shows that of the 31 shares, the rise–fall indicator gave the best selling price in 20 instances. However, as we mentioned earlier, this indicator tends to give its signal before the others, and this is borne out by Table 7.11, because for these 31 shares, in 30 instances the rise–fall indicator signalled before the others, and in the 31st case it gave its signal at

Table 7.11. The selling signals, prices and gains/losses for the 31 strongest shares in Table 6.4 since 5th May 1978

Share	Price at 5 May 1978	13-week average indicator			9-week low indicator			Rise-fall indicator		
		Date	Price	Gain (loss)	Date	Price	Gain (loss)	Date	Price	Gain (loss)
Automated Security	79	no signal			no signal			6 Apr. 79	133	68.35
Prince of Wales	53	19 May 79	105	98.11	27 Apr. 79	113	113.21	9 Dec. 78	90	69.81
Neil & Spencer	102	28 Oct. 78	108	5.88	6 Oct. 78	120	17.65	25 Aug. 78	122	19.61
Homecharm	148	no signal		156.80	no signal	156.8	5.95	11 Nov. 78	210	41.89
Hoveringham	77	26 Jan. 79	86	11.69	25 Nov. 78	87	12.99	6 Oct. 78	88	14.29
Johnson Cleaners	100	28 Oct. 78	91	−9.00	28 Oct. 78	91	−9.00	18 Aug. 78	101	1.00
Monk	100	25 Nov. 78	96	−4.00	11 Nov. 78	96	−4.00	4 Nov. 78	98	−2.00
Centreway	242	28 July 79	333	37.60	29 Sept. 78	257	6.20	8 Sept. 78	278	14.88
Horizon	106	no signal		145.30	no signal		145.30	1 Sept. 78	103	−2.83
Brooker Tool	32	11 Nov. 78	40	25.00	21 Oct. 78	42	31.25	18 Aug. 78	48	50.00
Shermans	12.5	15 Sept. 78	13.5	8.00	22 Sept. 78	13	4.00	18 Aug. 78	14	12.00
Securicor	98	9 Sept. 78	122	24.49	4 Nov. 78	120	22.45	25 Aug. 78	133	35.71
Forminster	102	11 Nov. 78	102	.00	18 Nov. 78	101	−.98	25 Aug. 78	104	1.96
Maple	19	4 Nov. 78	20.5	7.89	4 Nov. 78	20.5	7.89	1 Sept. 78	21.5	13.16
Reed Executive	52	19 June 79	79	51.92	26 Jan. 79	76.5	47.12	8 Sept. 78	69	32.69
United Scientific	322	28 Oct. 78	312	−3.11	13 Oct. 78	336	4.35	1 Sept. 78	362	12.42
Johnson Richards	130	29 Sept. 78	132	1.54	29 Sept. 78	132	1.54	8 Sept. 78	136	4.62
John Brown	324	4 Nov. 78	415	28.09	28 Oct. 78	425	31.17	29 Sept. 78	435	34.26
Electrocomponents	199	29 Jan. 79	423	112.56	4 Nov. 78	275	38.19	22 Sept. 78	309	55.28
Arthur Bell	256	1 Sept. 78	237	−7.42	1 Sept. 78	237	−7.42	1 Sept. 78	237	−7.42
Time Products	136	4 Nov. 78	175	28.68	4 Nov. 78	175	28.68	18 Aug. 78	192	41.18
Comet Radiovision	122	28 Oct. 78	136	11.48	28 Oct. 78	136	11.48	1 Sept. 78	149	22.13
Carlton Industries	185	4 Nov. 78	210	13.51	28 Oct. 78	218	17.84	22 Sept. 78	232	25.41
Gieves Group	101	28 Oct. 78	90	−10.89	28 Oct. 78	90	−10.89	11 Aug. 78	97	−3.96
Dobson Park	83	28 Oct. 78	102	22.89	28 Oct. 78	102	22.89	25 Aug. 78	114	37.35
Metalrax	45	11 Nov. 78	48	6.67	4 Nov. 78	48	6.67	29 Sept. 78	52	15.56
Rosgill	14	no signal		121.40	no signal		121.40	29 Sept. 78	22	57.14
Grand Metropolitan	113	1 Sept. 78	112	−.88	29 Sept. 78	110	−2.65	1 Sept. 78	112	−.88
George Ewer	28	13 Oct. 78	36	28.57	1 Sept. 78	34.5	23.21	8 June 78	36.5	30.36
MFI	78	no signal		387.20	no signal		387.20	1 Sept. 78	131	67.95
Whitbread	99	18 Aug. 78	120	21.21	18 Aug.	120	21.21	1 Sept. 78	125	26.26
Average Gain				45.31			38.01			25.42

the same time as the 13-week moving average (Grand Metropolitan). Looking at the performance of each of the indicators, the rise–fall indicator gave an overall gain for the 31 shares of 27.9%. Using the 13-week moving average method, the overall gain was 49.0%, while using the 9-week low method, the overall gain was 46.7%. On balance, therefore, the 13-week moving average turns out to be the best indicator for the whole group of shares, and the rise–fall indicator appears to be the worst. This picture is not quite as clear-cut as it seems, because the reason for the overall gain on the rise–fall indicator being lower is that it got us out of five shares for which the other indicators did not give a signal during the following year. Therefore in those instances, where there was a selling signal generated by all three indicators during the course of the year, the rise–fall indicator then turns out to be the best.

At first glance the overall best gain of 49% (moving average indicator) may look extremely disappointing when compared with the 76.3% gain calculated for the top 31 shares had they been held for exactly 1 year. This might even lead us to the conclusion that we could do without a selling indicator altogether and sell our shares 1 year after we buy them! There are, though, two main reasons why the performance in terms of gains and losses, as shown in Table 7.11, when a selling indicator is used, is superior to the gains and losses shown in Table 6.5, when an indicator is not used and we simply hold the shares for a specified time.

1. The *risk* in holding these shares has greatly reduced. In Table 6.5 it can be seen that two shares lost 25.8 and 17.7% respectively over the 1-year period. With a small portfolio there is some chance that one or both of these shares are held, together with a few others with small gains, so that the overall portfolio is in a losing situation. From Table 7.11, selling at the times indicated would have resulted in losses in four shares. However, the losses themselves were of 0.9, 2.0, 2.8 and 4.2% respectively, which can almost be considered to be of negligible proportions. Correct selling has therefore reduced the risk of loss for those shares which fail to come up to expectations.
2. Although the overall gain for the 31 shares is less, the gain has been accumulated over a shorter time period than the 1-year period given in Table 6.5. The average period of time for which 31 shares were held before selling according to the indicators was 19 weeks, i.e. about 4 1/2 months. A gain of 27.9% over this period, if compounded to a 1-year period at the same rate of gain, is equivalent to an annual gain of more than 97%!

Because of changes in the shares which are selected on the basis of volatility and strength, as discussed in Chapter 6, it is essential that a new list be prepared during each market fall. It is not so important to prepare a new list of the 100 or so most volatile shares if two buying opportunities arise within a short time of each other, as sometimes occurs (e.g. in 1978 and 1979) but it is still necessary to recalculate the strongest shares for the second occasion, since these will differ substantially from those listed for the first occasion.

Although it is impressive to show that the gain obtained by correct buying and selling of the 31 shares in Table 7.11 would have compounded to an annual gain of about 97%, this does not really tell us how effective these indicators are in getting us out near the peak price. Half of the gain we made may be said to be due to correct buying, while the other half is due to correct selling. A good way to evaluate the selling indicators is to use the methods we applied to the Babcock and John Brown shares, in which we calculated how far down, percentagewise, from the peak price, the indicators told us to sell.

Since we have already decided, based on the information in Table 7.11, that the rise–fall indicator was superior in those cases where all three of the indicators gave a selling signal, we need only give the results for that indicator. This is done, for the 31 shares, in Table 7.12. Under the heading 'Percentage down from peak price' the smaller the value the better, since of course a figure of 0 would mean that we sold at the exact top. Such a figure would not, of course, be obtainable since we never know a peak price was a peak price until after we have passed it and are already on the way down. Ideally, we would like to be told to sell when we were somewhere between 5 and 10% back from the peak—anything less than 5%, consistently, is unrealistic.

The average 'percentage down from the peak price' for the 31 shares in Table 7.12 is 7.8%, which is an impressive performance. This means that, for an average share which reaches a peak price of 100p before falling back, say to 50p, the indicator would have told us to sell at a price of 92p, and thus would have saved most of the profit we achieved from buying that share in the first place.

The most successful instance for the working of the selling indicator was the case of Electrocomponents, when we would have got out only 1.1% down from the peak price—selling at 96p when the peak was 97p. The least successful was Rosgill, where we would have been told to sell 29% down from the peak price. In the table there are six shares in which the rise–fall indicator appeared to be less successful than one would hope. These are John Brown, Prince of Wales Hotels, Horizon, Reed Executive, Rosgill and George Ewer. They bear closer examination because, in fact, the performance of the indicator in these cases is not as bad as would at first appear. In none of these instances did the indicator allow profits to dwindle away. What happened was the indicator got us out too soon and the share price

Table 7.12. Trigger points of the rise—fall indicator

Share	Peak price (p)	Price when indicator signalled	Percentage down from peak price
Automated Security	145	133	8.3
Prince of Wales	125	90	28.0
Neil & Spencer	131	122	6.9
Homecharm	230	210	8.7
Hoveringham	90	88	2.2
Johnson Cleaners	110	101	8.2
Monk	107	98	8.4
Centreway	295	278	5.8
Horizon	121	103	14.9
Brooke Tool	50	48	4.0
Shermans	14.5	14	3.4
Securicor	135	133	1.5
Forminster	108	104	3.7
Maple	22.5	21.5	4.4
Reed Executive	80	69	13.8
United Scientific	379	362	4.5
Johnson Richards	143	136	4.9
John Brown	490	435	11.2
Electrocomponents	312.5	309	1.1
Arthur Bell	260	237	8.8
Time Products	206	192	6.8
Comet Radiovision	164	149	3.2
Carlton Industries	235	232	1.3
Gieves Group	102	97	4.9
Dobson Park	117	114	2.6
Metalrax	55	52	5.5
Rosgill	31	22	29.0
Grand Metropolitan	119.5	112	6.3
George Ewer	46	36.5	20.7
MFI	146	131	10.3
Whitbread	135	125	7.4
			Average = 7.8%

recovered and moved to an even greater high. The percentages in Table 7.12 for these shares are, therefore, unrealistic in the sense that they refer to the eventual peak top, which may have occurred months later.

In two cases, Prince of Wales Hotels and Reed Executive, the indicator gave a selling signal on what was a considerable fall in price but was of sufficiently short duration that the 13-week moving average and 9-week low signals were, therefore, not triggered. The latter was triggered some months later. The rise—fall indicator would have got us out within 2.2% for Prince of Wales Hotels and 5.2% for Reed Executive of the minor peak top, and hence the indicator can be said to have been very effective. As far as George Ewer, Horizon and Rosgill are concerned, the indicator was less satisfactory, shaking us out after what turned out to be a fairly minor drop in the share price. In the case of John Brown the fall was so rapid that we were 11.2% down from the peak top before the indicator was triggered. Even so, the rise–fall indicator was still superior to both the 13-week moving average and the 9-week low method in that particular instance.

If we replace the values for Prince of Wales Hotels and Reed Executive in Table 7.12 by the figures of 2.2 and 5.2%, for the reasons we have just outlined, that we were dealing with a peak on a peak as it were, then the average value of 7.8% for the 30 shares comes down to 6.6%.

Now we have looked more closely at the working of the rise–fall indicator, we can form a much clearer impression of how it has worked for the 31 shares. For 26 of the shares the indicator worked superbly. For the other five cases it worked as a failsafe device, getting us out of a situation which looked threatening at the time and which might have led to a serious fall in price. In no cases did it leave us holding a share which plummeted from what was the peak price at the time. We can expect no more from any selling indicator, and can, quite obviously, apply this indicator with confidence to our entire shareholding.

Since, as has been mentioned earlier, only the moving average and 9-week low indicators are convenient for calculation by microcomputer, it is of interest to see how these indicators have worked when applied to the selection of strong shares made during the 1984 market, as given in Table 6.9 previously. The results of doing this are shown in Table 7.13. The average gain obtained by using the 13-week moving average was 36.1%, while for the 9-week low method a gain of 35.1% was obtained. There were three shares which had not given a selling signal by the time of writing (11th May 1985): Lamont (160.3% gain), Illingworth (147.0% gain), Gratton (131.1% gain) and Cronite (123.2% gain). Since these were the four shares with the highest gains in Table 6.9, it is important to have an indicator, such as these two, which does not get you out prematurely from the high-flying shares.

The sale of one share was triggered by the 9-week low and not the average, while five shares had sales triggered by the moving average and not the 9-week low.

A study of the triggering of shares by the moving average and 9-week lows in Table 7.11 for the 1978 market and in Table 7.13 for the 1984 market shows that slightly superior results can be obtained by waiting for both the 13-week moving average and the 9-week low to give their signals, and not to sell on the first signal from whichever indicator. This resulted in an improvement of about 2% in the gains achieved for the shares listed in Table 7.11, and about 4% for those shares listed in Table 7.13.

As has been mentioned earlier, microcomputers are ideal for the storage, retrieval and calculation of 13-week averages and 9-week lows, and Table 7.14 gives an example of such a printout for Henriques and Booker-McConnel share prices between 5th October 1984 and 1st February 1985.

The selling signals and gains and losses for the shares in Table 6.5 since August 1984

Share	Price at 3 Aug. 1984	13-week average indicator			9-week low indicator		
		Date	Price	Gain (loss)	Date	Price	Gain (loss)
Henriques	87	9 Nov. 84	82	-5.75	19 Oct. 84	80	-8.05
Booker McConnel	177	19 Apr. 85	248	40.11	—	257	45.20
Canning (W.)	163	9 Nov. 84	104	-36.20	26 Oct. 84	107	-34.36
Ryan Hotels	14	19 Apr. 85	24.5	75.00	—	26.5	89.29
Lincroft	105	18 Jan. 85	144	37.14	18 Jan. 85	144	37.14
Manganese Bronze	57	16 Nov. 84	56	-1.75	16 Nov. 84	56	-1.75
Leech William	115	12 Apr. 85	174	51.30	—	174	51.30
Arcolectric	31	25 Jan. 85	46	48.39	4 Jan. 85	44	41.94
CASE	205	25 Jan. 85	275	34.15	4 Jan. 85	294	43.41
Cronite	21.5	—	48	123.26	—	48	123.26
Glanfield Lawr.	55	14 Dec. 84	52	-5.45	25 Jan. 85	51	-7.27
Liberty	270	—	530	96.30	—	530	96.30
Rotaflex	114	26 Apr. 85	146	28.07	26 Apr. 85	146	28.07
Comb. English	74	—	128	72.97	—	128	72.97
Fujitsu	402	28 Dec. 84	450	11.94	7 Dec. 84	452	12.44
Ward Holdings	132	30 Nov. 84	135	2.27	1 Feb. 85	127	-3.79
Renold	36.5	26 Oct. 84	45	23.29	26 Oct. 84	45	23.29
Allebone	39	19 Oct. 84	37	-5.13	26 Oct. 84	35.5	-8.97
Lamont	58	—	151	160.34	—	151	160.34
Cory (Horace)	30.5	14 Dec. 84	33	8.20	—	41	34.43
Emray	19.25	4 Jan. 85	16.75	-12.99	25 Jan. 85	16.25	-15.58
Downiebrae	43	18 Jan. 85	21	-51.16	—	22	-48.84
Ellis & Goldstone	54	1 Mar. 85	76	40.74	—	80	48.15
Croda	120	12 Apr. 85	135	12.50	5 Apr. 85	133	10.83
Chloride	33	—	37	12.12	19 Oct. 84	30	-9.09
Grattan	90	—	208	131.11	—	208	131.11
Cosalt	69	9 Nov. 84	59	-14.49	9 Nov. 84	59	-14.49
Christie-Tyler	41	3 May 85	43	4.88	5 Apr. 85	42	2.44
Illingworth M.	34	—	84	147.06	—	84	147.06
Hogg Robinson	180	—	280	55.56	2 Nov. 84	197	9.44
				Average gain = 36.13			Average gain = 35.21

Table 7.14. Example of a computerized price and moving average calculation

Microvest + report

Date		Henriques	Av: 13 wk	Booker	Av: 13 wk
5 Oct.	84	88	83.23077	188	177.2308
12 Oct.	84	90	84.84615	186	179.2308
19 Oct.	84	80	85.61539	177	180.1538
26 Oct.	84	84	86.76923	199	182.3077
2 Nov.	84	84	87.69231	216	185.4615
9 Nov.	84	82	87.46154	213	187.8462
16 Nov.	84	80	86.46154	219	191.3077
23 Nov.	84	80	85.30769	208	194.3077
30 Nov.	84	73	84.38461	203	195.9231
7 Dec.	84	70	83.23077	206	197.6923
14 Dec.	84	68	81.76923	222	200.6154
21 Dec.	84	66	79.61539	220	203.3077
28 Dec.	84	64	77.61539	220	205.9231
4 Jan.	85	60	75.46154	223	208.6154
11 Jan.	85	54	72.69231	242	212.9231
18 Jan.	85	58	71	253	218.7692
25 Jan.	85	52	68.53846	266	223.9231
1 Feb.	85	52	66.07692	255	226.9231

Computer programs for this are available commercially, and for those investors who do not wish to become involved with microcomputers, there is a service available to provide the investor with the results of such computations (see Appendix B).

Chapter 8

The Method in Practice

At this point in the book it is necessary to take stock of the methods we have developed so far in separate chapters, and show how they link together in one rounded package. We can also indicate the steps we have to take each weekend in order to keep on top of market developments, so that a reader could, from the information in this chapter alone, function as an investor who regularly outperforms the market, as measured by either the Financial Times Index or the All Share Index.

The essentials of the method are these:

1. We have developed a buying indicator which measures the state of the market and tells us to buy within a few weeks of the market climate changing for the better. This indicator has, over the past decade, consistently marked the beginning of upward surges in share prices that have lasted for at least a few months.
2. We have developed a method of choosing shares which, from the buying signal onwards, outperform the market in general.
3. We have developed an indicator to tell us when to sell the shares we have bought. Over the past decade this indicator has told us to sell when the share price has been an average of about 7–8% down from the peak price. About once in every four or five occasions the indicator gives a selling signal for a share which later recovers and moves to new heights. This is the price we pay for added safety, because this indicator has rarely allowed us to ride a share price down more than 10% from its peak price.

To show what we have to do each week in practice, we can assume that the market is falling when we commence the method. This allows us to pass throught the above categories 1–3 consecutively.

MEASURING THE MARKET

(**Time**: 5 minutes each week)

Each week we keep a record of the Friday closing value of the Financial Times Index and from these we can calculate a 5-week and 13-week moving average. The best method of recording this information, and later the information on individual share prices is to use A4 paper ruled into 5 mm squares, obtainable from any stationers. For the market index we can rule eight vertical columns headed 'Date', 'FT Index', '5-week take away', '5-week total', '5-week average', '13-week take away', '13-week total' and finally '13-week average'. The 'take away' columns need only be one square wide, since only crosses will be put into them to remind us which value of the index to subtract from the 5-week and 13-week running totals. All the other columns can be five squares wide. Figure 8.1 shows a typical record of this type. We cannot compute a 5-week average until we have recorded five weekly values of the FT Index, and we cannot compute a 13-week average until we have 13 weeks' values of the index.

The 5-week average is calculated as follows. Once we have five consecutive weeks' values of the Index, add these and put the total in the '5-week total' column on the same horizontal line as the week 5. Dividing this by 5 gives us the 5-week average, which is put in the appropriate column again opposite week 5. On the sixth week, we have to subtract the FT Index value for week 1 from this total, and add in the value for week 6. This is where the 'take away' column comes in. In this column, opposite week 1,

DATE	FT INDEX	X	5 WK TOTAL	5 WK AVGE	X	13 WK TOTAL	13 WK AVGE
5.1.80	413.9	X	2086.1	417.2	X	5577.1	429.0
12.1.80	415.2	X	2106.1	421.2	X	5557.3	425.9
19.1.80	459.8	X	2146.3	428.6	X	5527.3	425.2
26.1.80	452.4	X	2179.1	435.8	X	5539.5	426.1
2.2.80	447.8	X	2209.1	441.8	X	5555.6	427.4
9.2.80	461.4	X	2256.6	451.2	X	5596.1	430.5
16.2.80	452.6	X	2284.0	456.8	X	5651.7	434.7
23.2.80	454.2	X	2278.4	455.6	X	5697.3	438.3
1.3.80	467.1	X	2293.1	458.6	X	5743.7	441.8
8.3.80	455.7	X	2301.0	460.2	X	5783.8	444.9
15.3.80	439.9	X	2279.5	455.8		5804.1	446.5
22.3.80	429.9	X	2246.8	449.2		5814.4	447.3
29.3.80	421.5	X	2214.1	442.8		5818.1	447.5
5.4.80	432.6	X	2179.6	435.9		5836.8	449.0
12.4.80	435.6	X	2159.5	431.8		5897.2	449.0
19.4.80	442.7	X	2169.3	432.4		5820.1	447.7
26.4.80	427.5	X	2159.9	431.8		5795.2	445.8
3.5.80	443.6	X	2182.0	436.4		5791.0	445.5
10.5.80	436.5		2186.0	437.2		5766.1	443.5
17.5.80	435.7		2186.0	437.2		5739.2	441.5
24.5.80	423.3		2166.6	433.3		5708.3	439.1
31.5.80	415.9		2155.0	431.0		5657.2	435.2
7.6.80	428.5		2134.9	426.0		5690.0	433.1

Figure 8.1. The weekly data kept on the Financial Times Index.

i.e. the week which we have subtracted from the total, we put across. Finally, the new running total 'week 5 total − week 1 index + week 6 index' goes into the '5-week total' column opposite week 6, and this total, divided by 5 goes into the '5-week average' column.

Next week, week 7, we take the latest running total, and subtract the FT Index after the one with a cross and add in the latest week 7 value of the Index, and just continue in this fashion.

The 13-week average is calculated in exactly the same way, adding up the first 13 weeks' value of the Index to give the first total and average. On week 14 we take away the Index for week 1, put a cross in the '13-week take away' column, and add in the Index for week 14. Dividing this by 13 gives the 13-week average. This procedure is continued for subsequent weeks.

Depending on whether you think you are an aggressive investor or more cautious, your buying signal is given when either the 5-week average, which has been falling so far, turns upward, or when the 13-week average also turns upward.

DECIDING WHAT TO BUY

(a) Listing volatile shares

(**Time**: 1–2 hours, once during a falling market)
When the 13-week average has been falling some months, it is time to prepare a list of the 100–150 or so most volatile shares from all those in the *Financial Times* list of shares. Go through the columns marked '1979/80' or whichever year is recorded there 'high and low'. Underline all those shares which a mental calculation shows that the ratio of high to low prices is about 1.5 or more. If you have 100–150 such shares, all well and good, if many more, raise the required ratio to 1.6 or 1.7 as necessary to keep below 150. If the number is less than 100, lower the required ratio a little. This choosing operation should take no more than 30 minutes. The rest of the time comes in writing these shares down. Again, our 5 mm squared paper is useful for this. Rule it off vertically in columns headed 'share', '1979/80 high', '1979/80 low' (change the year as appropriate) 'Price at—', 'Price at—as % of 1979/80 high'. This gives five columns, only three of which (share and high, low prices) we can use at the moment to write in the volatile shares we have chosen. The—will have the data entered when the market, as signalled by the indicator we are following, turns up.

(b) Choosing strong shares

(**Time**: 1–2 hours, once when the market indicator turns up)
Once the 5-week average or 13-week average of the Financial Times Index turns up—depending upon which you are using as your buying indicator—it

is time to choose the strongest shares from the list of volatile shares. Enter into the list of volatile shares the prices for the week the average turns up. For each share, calculate its price as a percentage of the price in the 1979/80 (or whichever year is entered) 'high' column, and enter this value in the appropriate column.

If the market has not fallen very far from its previous high, quite a proportion of the shares in the list will show percentage values greater than 100%, whereas for a drastic fall in the market, only a few, or perhaps none, will have risen higher than their previous high.

Finally, make a list of the 30 strongest shares in this list. Your selection of five or six shares to buy is then made from this list.

DECIDING WHEN TO SELL

(**Time**: 15 minutes each week)
Once you have bought shares, continue to keep track of the FT Index by means of the 13-week moving average, since this is your guide to general market conditions. However, your main attention now turns to the performance of the shares you have bought. It will be necessary to keep track of three indicators, the 13-week average, 9-week low and the rise–fall indicator. Be means of the 5 mm squared paper, all the data for a share can be collected on one sheet of paper. The paper can be ruled off in columns for 'Date', 'Price', '13-week take away', '13-week total', '13-week average' and '9-week low'. If these columns are kept to the left hand half of the page, the rise–fall indicator can be plotted on the right-hand half of the paper. An example is shown in Fig 8.2.

The 13-week average for the share is kept in exactly the same way as that for the FT Index. The 9-week low indicator simply means that each week we enter the lowest price that the share reached during the previous 9 weeks. The rise–fall indicator is started for the first week on the line for week 1, on one of the 5 mm ruled lines about halfway across the right hand half of the page. If the price falls the following week, draw a line to the next 5 mm square on the left, if the price rises, draw it to the right, while if the price remains the same, draw the line vertically down to the next ruled line. Figure 8.2 should make clear how this indicator is maintained. Once we have one or more 'saw teeth' we can draw a trend line through the bottom of the teeth.

Selling signals are generated when the 13-week average turns down, when the price drops lower than the lowest price in the last 9 weeks, and when the trend-line of the rise–fall indicator is violated on the downside.

The proceeds from sales of shares should not be reinvested in shares until the next turn up in the market is signalled by the 13-week moving average of the FT Index.

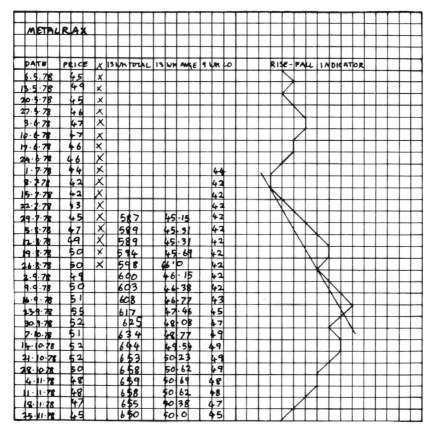

METALRAX

DATE	PRICE	X	13 WK TOTAL	13 WK AVGE	9 WK LO	RISE-FALL INDICATOR
6.5.78	45	X				
13.5.78	49	X				
20.5.78	45	X				
27.5.78	46	X				
3.6.78	47	X				
10.6.78	47	X				
17.6.78	46	X				
24.6.78	46	X				
1.7.78	44	X			44	
8.7.78	42	X			42	
15.7.78	42	X			42	
22.7.78	43	X			42	
29.7.78	45	X	587	45.15	42	
5.8.78	47	X	589	45.31	42	
12.8.78	49	X	589	45.31	42	
19.8.78	50	X	594	45.69	42	
26.8.78	50	X	598	46.0	42	
2.9.78	49		600	46.15	42	
9.9.78	50		603	46.38	42	
16.9.78	51		608	46.77	43	
23.9.78	55		617	47.46	45	
30.9.78	52		625	48.08	47	
7.10.78	51		634	48.77	49	
14.10.78	52		644	49.54	49	
21.10.78	52		653	50.23	49	
28.10.78	50		658	50.62	49	
4.11.78	48		659	50.69	48	
11.11.78	48		658	50.62	48	
18.11.78	47		655	50.38	47	
25.11.78	45		650	50.0	45	

Figure 8.2 The weekly data kept once a share has been bought.

With the spread of microcomputers into all areas of life, these devices offer a way of not only reducing the time available to store the above information on shares but to retrieve the information rapidly. Two hundred or more shares can readily be kept track of weekly by this means. More information on their availability and programmes relevant to investors is given in Appendix E.

The overall effect we are aiming to achieve with this investment method is shown in Fig. 8.3. When the market is rising, we hope to be rising with it, giving us a large capital gain. Some of this will be lost by virtue of the fact that our selling indicators only tell us to sell when our shares have come off their tops. Our capital will then stand still, or gain at bank deposit or building society rates of interest if we do place it, while the market falls. On the next rise we step aboard again, and so on. It will not take too many such operations to double, treble or multiply by even more our original starting capital.

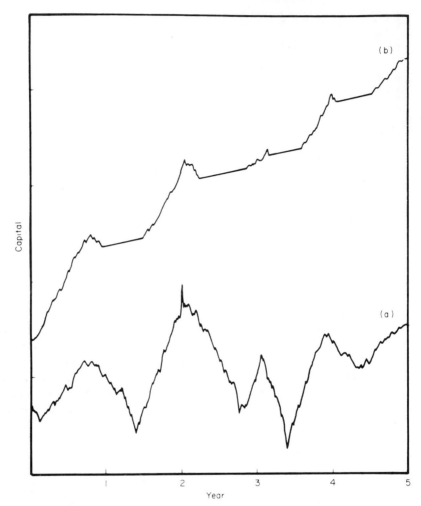

Figure 8.3. How we hope our capital will grow: (a) the behaviour of a typical stock market; (b) the behaviour of our investments over the same period of time.

Chapter 9

What to Do if the Market is Falling

The short answer to the question 'What should I do if the market is falling?' is 'Nothing!' Nothing, that is, besides collect data about the most volatile shares, and those amongst these volatile shares that are the strongest according to the rules outlined in the last chapter, and of course keep track of the 5-week and 13-week moving averages of the Financial Times Index in order to determine when to come into the market. If you are new to investment when you pick up this book, then undoubtedly you will be impatient to get started. After all, who wants to have to wait a year perhaps until the market rises again before making the first investment decision? If you really must take the plunge, there are several procedures which one can utilize to make investments in a falling market, but such investments are of necessity subject to higher risk than the methods which have been discussed so far in this book. This should be clearly understood, as should the fact that the procedures are not short-term, so that one's money could be tied up for a number of years before a profit is there for the taking. If you have some money available now which you would like to invest, but see yourself needing it next year or the year after to buy a car, boat, or build that extension you have been after for so long, then skip this chapter, since you will find yourself having to sell your shares at the time when you are showing the greatest loss. Only if you have some uncommitted capital should you envisage applying the methods discussed in this chapter.

Besides money, one thing that you should have available to supply at the outset is strong nerve, because you are going to be asked to invest a sum of money, watch the value of your investment go down, and then be asked to buy even more of the same shares. It sounds very much like throwing good money after bad. However, the type of share that we are going to invest is a cyclical one, that has fluctuated fairly widely in price on a fairly long-term scale, peaking out every 4 years or even longer. So, however badly it is doing at the moment, we can reasonably expect that, some time in the not too distant future, the price is going to rise sufficiently to give us a profit. We wish to accumulate a large number of these shares when the price is falling, and the lower the price falls the better. The element of risk involved is the degree of uncertainty that the price will ever rise again above what we have paid for the shares. If it does not, then we will lose money. If they rise even higher than their previous peak, then we will make a very good profit. Bearing in mind the time-scale we are talking about, it could well be 4 or 5 years before we see that profit. Because of this long time interval we should hope to achieve a profit of at least 100% over a 4-year period in order to improve on the methods developed in the previous chapters of this book

Each of the methods illustrated here employs the principle of cost averaging. We have to buy shares at fixed intervals which we decide on ourselves, bearing in mind our cash flow situation.

The prevailing share price at the allotted time must not affect our decision to buy—there must be no question of saying to ourselves, 'Why not wait another week or so because the price is going to move in our favour?'. The buying must be completely automatic on the predetermined date. Once we have carried out a number of such purchases, the cost per share to us will start to approach the average value at which they have stood over the period of time. If we happen to be buying when the actual price is below the average, then that will tend to decrease our cost per share even further, so giving us a greater potential for profit when the rise comes. Our profit starts to appear when the price of the share rises above the average price, or rather above the price per share which we have paid by then.

Before we commence one of these schemes of investment we have to decide on two things: firstly, how much money we are going to have available over, say, the coming 4-year period, and secondly, which share we are going to buy.

As far as the money available is concerned, we should be buying our shares at a frequency of somewhat between 2 and 6 months, and we should bear in mind that it is not economical to invest less than about £150 at a time if commission is not to form an overly large percentage of the costs. So, the sort of investment that we have in mind is between say £300 and £1000 per year, over at least a 4-year period. As emphasized earlier, this type of operation should not be undertaken unless these funds are totally uncommitted. The last thing we want to have to do is to realize our investment when share prices are low, and, life being what it is, share prices will be low when we need the money most.

The criteria for selecting the share are that it should have a history of cyclicality, and that it should be as 'safe' a company as possible—although since the Rolls-Royce affair it is apparent that there is no such thing as a safe company. It will be fairly easy to choose such a company by reference to Appendix D at the end of this book, where a list of the FTSE-100 top companies are given. The example used in this chapter is that used in the previous edition of this book; John Brown, the engineering company. Although not now in the top 100 companies, the principles and procedure discussed in this chapter are applicable to any cyclical share, and John Brown is a very good example of cyclicality during the period in question, as can be seen from the chart of its share price from 1970 to 1979 given in Fig A.19.

For the purposes of these calculations we shall assume that an investment is made every 20 weeks, i.e. about every 5 months.

Method 1: buying a constant number of shares

In this method we buy a fixed number of shares, for example 100, 200, 1000 as the case may be, each time our schedule says to buy. Applied to the shares of John Brown, we get the figures shown in Table 9.1. Columns in the table give us the number of shares bought to date and their cost to date, from which we calculate the most important fact, which is the cost per share to date. Other columns give us the market value to date, which is obtained by multiplying the number of shares held by their present market price. The difference between the market value and the amount we have paid to date gives us the gain or loss situation, expressed as a percentage. The buying scheme was started on 28th January 1972, and by 11th July 1975 we had bought 1000 shares, at a cost of £1182.00. However, at that time the market value of the shares, then standing at 60p, was only £600.00, so we were showing a loss of nearly 50% on our investment! That is the time for strong nerves, and is also a reason why we have said that we must not be in a position of needing this money and hence having to sell out at such a large loss. The system was vindicated by June 1977 when we moved into a profit. By May 1979 we had gained a very large profit indeed, our total expenditure of £3007.00 now being worth £10 640.00, showing a gain of 253.8% over the 7-year period from January 1972. In the figures presented here we have made no allowance for the commission involved in buying the share but have made the reasonable assumption that this would have been offset several times over by dividends received, so that the real gain would have been slightly higher than that shown.

This gain of 253% is far and away above that which we would have obtained by depositing the same sums in the building society or bank account

STOCKS AND SHARES SIMPLIFIED

Table 9.1. The long-term gain achieved by buying a constant number of shares in John Brown at constant intervals since 1972

Date	Price (p)	No. bought	Cumulative cost (£)	Total no. of shares held	Cost per share (p)	Value of investment (£)	Gain (loss)
28 Jan. 72	175	100	175	100	175	175	—
16 June 72	150	100	325	200	162.5	300	(7.7)
3 Nov. 72	135	100	460	300	153.3	405	(12.0)
23 Mar. 73	150	100	610	400	152.5	600	(1.7)
10 Aug. 73	155	100	765	500	153	775	1.3
28 Dec. 73	125	100	890	600	148.3	750	(15.7)
17 May 74	73	100	963	700	137.6	511	(46.9)
4 Oct. 74	77	100	1040	800	130	616	(40.8)
21 Feb. 75	82	100	1122	900	124.7	738	(34.2)
11 July 75	60	100	1182	1000	118.2	600	(49.2)
28 Nov. 75	60	100	1242	1100	112.9	660	(46.9)
16 Apr. 76	87	100	1329	1200	110.75	1044	(21.4)
3 Sept. 76	90	100	1419	1300	109.2	1170	(17.5)
21 Jan. 77	102	100	1521	1400	108.6	1428	(6.1)
10 June 77	200	100	1721	1500	114.7	3000	74.3
28 Oct. 77	205	100	1926	1600	120.4	3280	70.3
17 Mar. 78	276	100	2202	1700	129.5	4692	113.1
4 Aug. 78	430	100	2632	1800	146.2	7740	194.1
22 Dec. 78	375	100	3007	1900	158.3	7125	136.9
11 May 79	560	—	3007	1900	158.3	10640	253.8

Table 9.2. The long-term loss achieved by buying a constant number of shares in a mythical share ('reverse' John Brown) at constant intervals since 1972

Price (p)	No. bought	Cumulative cost (£)	Total no. of shares held	Cost per share (p)	Value of investment (£)	Gain (loss)
560	100	560	100	560	560	—
375	100	935	200	467.5	750	(19.8)
430	100	1365	300	455	1290	(5.5)
276	100	1641	400	410.3	1104	(32.7)
205	100	1846	500	369.2	1025	(44.5)
200	100	2046	600	341.0	1200	(41.3)
102	100	2148	700	306.9	714	(66.8)
90	100	2238	800	279.8	720	(67.8)
87	100	2325	900	258.3	783	(66.3)
60	100	2385	1000	238.5	600	(74.8)
60	100	2445	1100	222.3	660	(73.0)
82	100	2527	1200	210.6	984	(61.1)
77	100	2604	1300	200.3	1001	(61.6)
73	100	2677	1400	191.2	1022	(61.8)
125	100	2802	1500	186.8	1875	(33.1)
155	100	2957	1600	184.8	2480	(16.1)
150	100	3107	1700	182.8	2550	(17.9)
135	100	3242	1800	180.1	2430	(25.0)
150	100	3392	1900	178.5	2850	(16.0)
175	—	3392	1900	178.5	3325	(2.0)

over the same period of time. We could not have even doubled our money in the time by such means. So, on the basis of the example given here, cost averaging appears to be a very useful way of building up capital.

Before we rush off and start buying, though, let us look a little more closely at the John Brown situation. We started when the share price was 175p, and we calculated our profit on the selling share price of 560p in 1979. We cannot expect too many shares to start with a certain price which rises to three times that at the end of 7 years. We can certainly hope to see some kind of rise because, as shown in Chapter 2, share prices are tending to rise over the long term. Of course there is just a chance that they may start to fall over the next 4 or 5 years, and so, to keep our persepective, we should look at the situation where the share price does not rise as high as the former peak. A convenient way of doing this is to generate an artificial share by reversing the prices of John Brown shares. We can say that the price started at 560p and ended at 175p. What happens by adopting the same investment procedure of buying 100 shares each time can be seen from Table 9.2. The value of our shares, accumulated through 19 forays into the market, is about 2% down on the amount we paid for them, excluding any consideration of commission.

This loss illustrates one of the major shortcomings of cost averaging where we buy a constant number of shares, which is that it does not succeed if the long-term underlying trend of the share price is downwards. The reason for this is that the procedure we have adopted is simply giving us an arithmetical average of the share price and, of course, when the long-term trend is downwards it is a mathematical necessity that the average share price is going to fall. The only chance we might have to make a profit in such situations is if the share price spurts above this average for a short term. If it does, we would be advised to terminate the scheme of investment.

Method 2: buying with a constant sum of money

The key to success in cost averaging operations is to lower the cost per share which we have paid, i.e. our total expenditure divided by the number of shares we have accumulated at the time. The obvious way to do this is to buy more shares when prices are low than when they are high. This can be done quite simply by, instead of buying a fixed number of shares each time, as in the last method, investing a fixed sum each time. Thus if the price of the share drops to half its previous value, we will be able to buy twice as many.

As far as the examples which we have chosen to illustrate the method are concerned, they are somewhat artificial in the sense that such an exercise will result in buying of numbers of shares such as 189. Brokers do not take too kindly to this, and much prefer round hundreds, although they are not too upset at multiples of 50. However, we can ignore this factor for the moment since we only intend to illustrate the advantages of fixed sum investment over fixed number investment.

In order to come somewhere near the last example in terms of the total amount of money invested, we will base our calculations on fixed investments of £200. The results are shown in Table 9.3. The figures are extremely impressive, showing £3800 invested in John Brown shares by this procedure become worth £18 351 by May 1979 when the share price was standing at 560p. This represents a gain of 383% for the period, which is over half as much again as the previous method yielded.

The crucial point about this second method of investment is not so much how it performs on John Brown shares relative to the first method, but how well it would perform on the 'reverse John Brown' shares, which started off at a high level and then failed to come up to that on recovery. The answer, as can be seen from Table 9.4, is that this method produces a gain of 47.4% for the 7-year period. This is quite a turn-around from the 2% loss produced by the first method, and shows that the investment of a fixed sum of money rather than the buying of a fixed number of shares is the way to success with a cost averaging system. Having found an improved system for cost averaging, we might ask ourselves if the improved method can be improved even further. Since the aim in any system is to reduce the cost per share of our accumulated holding, this is the area to look at. The second method was an improvement over the first method because it resulted in the purchase of more shares when prices were low than when they were high. To do even better, we need to buy an even greater number of shares when prices are low. This will need extra money, and this extra money can come from the purchase of fewer shares when prices are high than was the case with the last method. So, instead of investing say £200 when prices are high, we should put in perhaps £150, and put the remaining £50 into a reserve fund. We can use this reserve to spend more than £200 when prices are low. The only further point to be decided is how to calculate how many shares to buy each time we have to invest. A good way of doing this is to link the share price itself with our accumulated cost per share, so that if our cost per share is substantially higher than the current share price, we buy a larger number of shares in order to reduce it. Conversely, if the accumulated cost per share is lower than the current share price, then any purchase will raise our cost per share. Since our policy is also to accumulate as many shares as we can, we will have to buy a few shares in such a situation, but the number will be kept low. The basis of this method will be therefore to decide upon a certain amount to invest each time, and use only a part of it when prices are high, but supplement it from the reserve we build up to buy many more shares when prices are low.

Table 9.3. The long-term gain achieved by investing a fixed amount of money in John Brown shares since 1972

Date		Price (p)	Amount invested (£)	Cumulative cost (£)	No. bought	Total no. held	Cost per share (£)	Value of investment (£)	Gain (loss)
28 Jan.	72	175	200	200	114	114	175	199.5	—
16 June	72	150	200	400	133	247	161.9	370.5	(7.4)
3 Nov.	72	135	200	600	148	395	151.9	533.3	(11.1)
23 Mar.	72	150	200	800	133	528	151.5	792	(1.0)
10 Aug.	73	155	200	1000	129	657	152.2	1018.4	1.8
28 Dec.	73	125	200	1200	160	817	146.9	1021.3	(14.9)
17 May	74	73	200	1400	274	1091	128.3	796.4	(43.1)
4 Oct.	74	77	200	1600	260	1351	118.4	1040.3	(35.0)
21 Feb.	75	82	200	1800	244	1595	112.9	1307.9	(27.3)
11 July	75	60	200	2000	333	1928	103.7	1156.8	(42.2)
28 Nov.	75	60	200	2200	333	2261	97.3	1356.6	(38.3)
16 Apr.	76	87	200	2400	230	2491	96.3	2167.2	(9.7)
3 Sept.	76	90	200	2600	222	2713	95.8	2441.7	(6.1)
21 Jan.	77	102	200	2800	196	2909	96.2	2967.2	(6.0)
10 June	77	200	200	3000	100	3009	99.7	6018	100.6
28 Oct.	77	208	200	3200	96	3105	103.1	6458.4	101.8
17 Mar.	78	276	200	3400	72	3177	107.0	8768.5	157.9
4 Aug.	78	430	200	3600	47	3224	111.7	13863.2	285.1
22 Dec.	78	375	200	3800	53	3277	116.0	12288.8	223.4
11 May	79	560	—	3800	—	3277	116.0	18351.2	382.9

Table 9.4. The long-term gain achieved by investing a fixed amount in a mythical share ('reverse' John Brown) at constant intervals since 1972

Price (p)	Amount invested (£)	No. bought	Cumulative cost (£)	Total no. of shares held	Cost per share (p)	Value of investment (£)	Gain (loss)
560	200	36	200	36	555	201.6	–
375	200	53	400	89	449	333.8	(16.5)
430	200	47	600	136	441	584.8	(2.5)
276	200	72	800	208	385	574.1	(28.2)
205	200	98	1000	306	327	627.3	(37.3)
200	200	100	1200	406	296	812	(32.3)
102	200	196	1400	602	233	614	(56.1)
90	200	222	1600	824	194	741.6	(53.7)
87	200	230	1800	1054	171	917	(49.1)
60	200	333	2000	1387	144	832.2	(58.4)
60	200	333	2200	1720	128	1032	(53.1)
82	200	244	2400	1964	122	1610.5	(32.9)
77	200	260	2600	2224	117	1712.5	(34.1)
73	200	274	2800	2498	112	1823.5	(34.9)
125	200	160	3000	2658	113	3322.5	10.8
155	200	129	3200	2787	115	4319.9	35
150	200	133	3400	2920	116	4380	28.8
135	200	148	3600	3068	117	4141.8	15.1
150	200	133	3800	3201	119	4801.5	26.4
175	–	–	3800	3201	119	5601.8	47.4

Method 3: relating amount invested to share price movements

Since we are going to start this exercise when prices are falling, at least in the case of John Brown shares, then of course we need a reserve fund before we start. This can be done by putting £500 into the reserve, and using only £100 for the first purchase, putting the next £100 into the reserve as well, so that the latter stands at £600 for the second purchase. The simplest way of deciding how much to invest at the second purchase is to use a ratio of our current cost per share (for the second purchase this will be the share price at the time of the first purchase) to the current share price. All these transactions are shown in detail in Table 9.5. In order to clarify matters we will go through the first few buying operations.

Initially we buy £100 worth of shares at 175p. This buys us 57 shares. The remaining £100 or our planned £200-per-time investment is added to the reserve, bringing it up to £600. For the second purchase we use the ratio of the cost per share so far to the new share price to tell us how much to invest. The ratio of the cost per share to the second share price is 175 to 150, i.e. 1.17. So, we invest $1.17 \times £200 = £234$ for the second purchase. Since we plan to invest £200 each month, the extra £34 come from the reserve.

To show a situation where we add to the reserve, we can look at the two points when the share prices were 276p and 430p. When the price was 276p the cost per share was 92.6p. The ratio of 92.6p to 430p is 0.215. Hence $0.215 \times £200 = £44$ was invested. By proceeding in this way the method gave a gain of 425.5% over the same period as was covered in other methods of investment.

As far as our 'reverse' John Brown shares are concerned, the method is more successful than the previous ones, resulting in a gain of 81.9% (Table 9.6).

Besides the gains achieved by these various methods, another point of concern is how large the loss gets during the investment period before it turns into a profit. In the case of the 'ordinary' John Brown shares, the lowest points were for method 1, -49.2%, for method 2, -43.1%, and for method 3, -36.0%. So, as well as giving a superior gain for John Brown, method 3 also limited the loss during the time the shares were falling. For the 'reverse' John Brown shares, method method 1 gave maximum loss of 74.8%, method 2 gave 58.4% and method 3 gave 66.2%, so that method 3 came somewhere between methods 1 and 2 in this case.

The gains for both types of share for each of the three methods are summarized in Table 9.7. Also shown is an average gain for the two types of shares, since perhaps we could consider this to approximate a typical share. It can be seen that on all counts method 3 is superior, and so is to be preferred as a method of investment.

We have already mentioned the problem of buying shares in odd numbers

Table 9.5. The long-term gain obtained by investing a proportion of a £200 repetitive amount in John Brown shares and putting the residue into a reserve (the proportion is determined by the change in share price)

Price	Factor	Amount invested (£)	No. of shares bought	Total no. held	Total cost (£)	Cost per share (p)	Reserve (£)	Value of reserve + shares	Gain (loss)
—	—	—	—	—	—	—	500	500	—
175	—	100	57	57	100	175	600	700	—
150	1.16	232	155	212	332	156.6	568	886	(1.5)
135	1.16	232	172	384	564	146.9	536	1 054.4	(4.1)
150	0.98	196	130	514	760	147.9	540	1 043.7	(19.7)
155	0.96	191	123	637	951	149.3	549	1 536.4	2.4
125	1.07	214	171	808	1165	144.2	535	1 545	(9.1)
73	1.81	361	494	1302	1526	117.2	374	1 324.5	(30.3)
77	1.42	284	370	1672	1810	108.3	290	1 577.4	(24.9)
82	1.25	250	304	1976	2060	104.3	240	1 860.3	(19.1)
60	1.65	330	551	2527	2390	94.6	110	1 626.2	(34.9)
60	1.51	302	503	3030	2692	88.8	8	1 826	(32.4)
87	0.98	196	225	3255	2888	88.7	12	2 843.9	(1.9)
90	0.95	190	211	3466	3078	88.8	22	3 141.4	1.3
102	0.84	168	164	3630	3246	89.4	54	3 756.6	13.8
200	0.43	87	43	3673	3333	90.7	167	7 513	114.7
205	0.43	87	42	3715	3420	92.1	280	7 895.8	113.4
276	0.32	64	23	3738	3484	93.2	416	10 732.9	175.2
430	0.21	43	10	3748	3527	94.1	573	16 689.4	307.1
375	0.24	49	13	2761	3576	95.1	724	14 827.8	244.8
560	—	—	—	3761	3576	95.1	724	21 785.6	406.6

Table 9.6. The long-term gain obtained by investing a proportion of a £200 repetitive amount in mythical share ('reverse' John Brown) and putting the residue into a reserve (the proportion is determined by the change in share price)

Price	Factor	Amount invested (£)	No. of shares bought	Total no. held	Total cost (£)	Cost per share (p)	Reserve (£)	Value of reserve + shares	Gain (loss)
—	—	—	—	—	—	—	500	500	—
560	—	100	18	18	100	560	600	700	—
375	1.49	300	80	98	400	408	500	867.5	(3.6)
430	0.95	190	44	142	590	415	510	1120.6	1.8
276	1.50	300	109	251	890	354.6	410	1102.8	(15.2)
205	1.73	344	168	419	1234	294	266	1124.9	(25)
200	1.47	294	147	566	1528	270	172	1304	(23.9)
102	2.64	527	517	1083	2318	214	−155	949.7	(50)
90	2.38	475	528	1611	2793	173.4	−430	1010	(51.9)
87	1.99	398	458	2069	3191	154.2	−628	1172	(49)
60	2.57	514	857	2926	3705	126.6	−942	813.6	(67.5)
60	2.11	422	703	3629	4127	113.7	−1164	1013.4	(62.5)
82	1.38	277	338	3967	4404	111	−1241	2011.9	(30.6)
77	1.44	288	374	4341	4692	108.1	−1329	2013.6	(35.0)
73	1.48	296	406	4747	4988	105.1	−1425	2040.3	(38.2)
125	0.84	168	134	4881	5156	105.6	−1393	4708.3	34.5
155	0.68	136	88	4969	5292	106.5	−1329	6372.9	72.2
150	0.71	143	95	5064	5435	107.3	−1272	6324	62.2
135	0.79	159	118	5182	5594	108	−1231	5764.7	40.6
150	0.72	144	96	5278	5738	108.7	−1175	6742	56.9
175	—	—	—	5278	5738	108.7	−1175	8061.5	87.5

Table 9.7. The gains (percentages) achieved by employing each of methods 1, 2 and 3 to John Brown and 'Reverse' John Brown shares

	Method 1	Method 2	Method 3
John Brown	253.8	382.9	425.5
'Reverse' John Brown	− 2.0	47.4	81.9
'Average' share	125.9	215.2	253.7

rather than multiples of 50 or 100, and of course this would be one of the problems of applying method 3, since by its nature it will signal the purchase of odd numbers of shares. The only way round this problem is to round the number of shares calculated, either up or down to the nearest 50. If the factor works out at more than 1.0, then the number could be rounded upwards, whereas if it is less than 1.0 it can be rounded downwards. This has the effect of allowing the purchase of even more shares when the price is falling, and less when the price is rising, thereby decreasing the cost per share to a greater extent than is shown in Tables 9.5 and 9.6. By this means the gains obtained will be greater than those we have illustrated in Tables 9.5 and 9.6.

Chapter 10

Options

Once you have had a number of successful forays into the market, one aspect will probably start to irritate you. This is that the rewards for being right in your investment decisions are not all that high. Your timing may be perfect as far as finding the bottom of the market and the top of your share price are concerned, but your selection of shares, although outperforming the market, are unlikely to include, unless you are extremely lucky, those that rack up gains of hundreds of per cent in a year or less. There is no way of finding these supershares, one notable example in the last 10 years being Brown & Jackson, in which an investor putting in a few thousand pounds a year or so would now be sitting on a six-figure investment. By the straightforward techniques we have been discussing in this book so far, we will probably achieve gains of between 50 and 100% in those bull markets which we have talked about. There is a way, however, in which being right can result in huge gains, although the opposite is also true, that being wrong will cost you more than simply buying and selling shares, and that is in the options market, particularly the traded options market which has been in existence in London since 1978.

Excluding traded options for the moment, standard options are of two types: 'put' options and 'call' options. A call option gives the right to buy, and a put option the right to sell at a specific price within a certain time period. This is usually 1, 2 or 3 months. Besides single options, which are either put or call, one can take out a double option, giving the right to buy or sell.

The 'striking price', which is the price at which the security can be bought or sold between now and the future expiry date, is usually the present market price plus a few per cent more. The cost of taking out the option would be, in the case of a 3-month option, typically 10 to 15%. As examples, the share price followed by the 3-month call rate in parentheses for some selected shares at the time of writing as follows:

Barclays, 554(42); Glaxo, 1100(90); ICI, 742(50); Marks & Spencer, 115(10).

The option can be taken up at any time within the specified period, or alternatively you can do nothing, in which case the option lapses and you lose the money which you paid for it. The share price will have to rise or fall by an amount sufficient to clear all these costs before you make a profit by exercising the option. The great advantage of options is that they enable you to take a position in the market at limited expense, and the rewards can be considerable if the correct view of the market's behaviour in the coming months has been taken.

In this chapter we will be concerned with traded options. In this particular market one can actually sell the option itself, so that in fact the option has a market value which is constantly changing as the share price changes. Options give us the high leverage or gearing on our investment, in the sense that say a 20% rise in the share price can raise the value of the option by several hundred per cent. Obviously the rewards for being right are substantially higher than in the normal buying and selling of the shares themselves. Of course, leverage works both ways, so that you will have an increased loss if your view of the market is wrong. There are two ways of looking at this kind of leverage. If you are an out-and-out gambler you could commit as much money in the options market as you might have put into shares. You may then make several hundreds percentage gain if you are correct or, of course, you can lose the lot. The other, more sensible way of looking at it is that you can commit only a fraction of your available funds, and still hope to make as much profit as if you had invested the whole of your capital in the purchase of shares. It is this latter view of options that we are advocating in this chapter, and we will not be committing anything like the sums of money that we would be putting into the straightforward dealing in shares. After all, if your timing and selection go badly wrong and your shares fall substantially, you still have some prospect that eventually they will come back in value, even though it might take a year or more. While that is happening you could adopt the philosophical attitude that your losses are only paper ones. With options, because of the limited time element, we have no such prospect, so our losses are real ones.

One valuable aspect of options, which we shall see shortly, is that they enable you to either increase or decrease the risk to your portfolio, and so traded options are going to be a valuable part of our investment techiques.

The traded options market is expanding the whole time, and at the time of writing consists of the shares of 30 companies, plus one short-term gilt, one currency rate and the FTSE-100 Index. They are all listed in Table 10.1.

Table 10.1. The London Traded Options market: months in which new 9-month options are introduced

	July	October	January	April	
BP		Consol. Goldfields			Courtaulds
Commercial Union		GEC			Grand Metropolitan
ICI		Land Securities			Marks & Spencer
Shell		Trafalgar House			
	August	November	February	May	
BAT		Barclays			British Aerospace
British Telecom		Imperial Group			LASMO
Lonrho		P & O			Racal
RTZ		Vaal Reefs			Exch. 10% 1989
	June	September	December	March	
BTR		Beecham			Bass
De Beers		GKN			Hanson
Jaguar		Tesco			FT-SE100 Index
Sterling—US dollar					

Dealings in these options concern contracts, a contract giving the right to buy 1000 shares of the particular company at a fixed price. The options are designated by a month and a price, for example BP July 500. At the time of writing this gives the purchaser the right to buy, for each contract, 1000 shares in British Petroleum at any time between now and July 1985, at a price of 100p each. At any one time there are always three different expiry months available, for example BP. July, October and January, so that these are 3 months apart. Once we reach October that option expires, and a new option appears called the July option. When a new option appears it is always for 9 months ahead, and no longer-term ones are available on the traded options market. The options are continually rolling over, so that in 3 months time, what is now a 3-month option expires, the 6-month one will have become a 3-month option and the present 9-month becomes a 6-month, with a new 9-month option being introduced.

As far as the striking prices—sometimes called the exercise prices—are concerned, there will be, at the time of issue, some prices below the share price prevailing at the time, and some prices above the share price. If a share moves up or down a considerable amount, some of the prices will be discontinued as being inappropriate when next a new option is introduced. When we put together a company, a month and an exercise price, that is called a series. To use BP as an example, in May 1985 the following series were available: July 460, July 500, July 550, July 600, October 460, October 500, October 550, October 600, January 460, January 500, January 550, January 600. At the time, the actual share price fluctuated between 500 and 550p.

The prices of all these available series of options are given in those newspapers that carry extensive lists of share prices, and for a particular share the prices will be different for each series. The further ahead the expiry date of the option, the more expensive it will be compared with earlier dated options, since it is assumed that the greater length of time available will give the buyer a better chance of the share price moving ahead. The lower the striking price of a call option, the higher will be the price of a contract. Thus the cheapest contract on any particular day should be the short-term, high-striking price series, while the most expensive should be the low-striking price, long-term series.

Two expressions which are used in discussions of options are 'in the money' and 'out of the money'. In the money means that the striking price when you take out the call option is lower than the actual share price. Because of this, at the time of purchase not all of the money you have paid for the contract is at risk. Out of the money means that the striking price is above the current share price, and so all of your money is at risk. Hence out of the money contracts are more highly speculative than in the money ones, but naturally will be more highly geared.

So far we have only discussed the buying of contracts, but obviously, since we have a market, we must have sellers as well as buyers. The sellers are called writers of options, and they undertake to deliver the shares to you at the striking price if you exercise the option. As a writer you would receive the contract price less dealing costs. Of course you would only do this if you expected the share price to go down below the striking price, in which circumstances the holder of the option would not exercise it. So that we do not have situations where the writers of options cannot deliver the shares, writers have to lodge a margin with the market of either a quarter of the shares concerned, or the cash equivalent. So, as long as you deposit the cash, you do not actually have to have the shares, and you are what is known as a naked writer, as opposed to the covered writers who do have the shares. To be a naked writer is a dangerous state of affairs, since a dramatic rise in the share price would mean that the call option would eventually be exercised against you, and you would have the problem of needing to buy the necessary shares at the much higher price.

We mentioned earlier that options can be used to reduce the risk to your portfolio. They can do this in the sense that we can take one view of the market as far as our shareholding is concerned, but cover ourselves for the market moving the other way by buying or writing options. Thus, supposing we think that the market is going to fall, we could liquidate our investments, but buy options with, say, 5–10% of the proceeds. If the market then rises, we can then come in at the cheap prices by exercising the options, or at least sell the options to increase our capital. On the other hand, if we think the market is going to rise, but wish to cover ourselves for a fall, we have at least made some money in the form of the payment we received for the contracts. Unfortunately, the taxman does not recognize this laudable aspect of options, and does not allow you to carry a loss forward against profits. He is very happy, however, to tax you on your profits.

Since we hope that by the timing methods discussed in the last chapter we will more often be correct than not about our view of the market, then it is unlikely that we would need to look at options as a means of neutralizing risk. To us they will be a means of increasing our profits when all the signals say that the market is taking off.

In the first edition of this book we discussed the behaviour of shares and options during the 1979 upward market move. In order to confirm the principles which were successful in that market, it is also useful to follow share and option prices from the August 1984 market, which we have also discussed at length in Chapter 6 and Chapter 8. In Chapter 5 we pointed out that a buying signal was given by the 13-week average on 9th March 1979. Since the market peaked out on 4th May, it will be useful to compare the movement of a share price and the option prices in that share to a point just after the peak, say the week ending 11th May. The share prices and the offer prices of these option series which ran right through the period in question are given in Table 10.2. The extra leverage given by options is readily seen from the figures. It is worth commenting upon specific figures for the best and worst performing shares during the period in order to see if we can draw any conclusions.

The best performing share was Marks & Spencer, whose share price rose from 101p to 123p for a gain of 21.8%. Taking the options in Marks & Spencer for a direct comparison between shares and options, we find that the best performing Marks & Spencer option series was the July 100's series which moved from 10.5p to 27p for a gain of 173.1%. The least successful Marks & Spencer series was the October 80s which rose from 28p to 50p for a gain of 78.6%. The average gain for the six Marks & Spencer series was 115.8%. So, in the most favourable case amongst these options, the gain obtained from investing in them was about seven times as high as if we had bought and sold the shares themselves.

As far as the worst performing share was concerned, this was EMI, whose share price fell from 120p to 105p, i.e. a loss of 12.5%. The heaviest losing option series was the May 140 series, losing 93.8%. The average loss for the 12 series was 53.9%, between four and five times the loss which would have been suffered by tansactions in the share themselves. This should serve to remind us of the fact that high gearing works both ways—in forward and reverse.

A similar exercise for the wider number of options available in the 1984 market gives the list in Table 10.3. Here are given the share prices on 4th August 1984, a market turning point as defined in Chapter 5. Unfortun-

Table 10.2. Share prices and offer prices on 9 Mar. 1979 and 11 May 1979 on various series on the traded options market

Share	Ex price	July option price		Percentage gain (loss)	October option price		Percentage gain (loss)	Share price		Percentage gain (loss)
		9 Mar. 79	11 May 79		9 Mar. 79	11 May 79		9 Mar. 79	11 May 79	
BP	950	182	242	33.0	200	260	30.0	£11⅛	£12⅜	11.2
	1000	142	192	35.2	162	215	32.7			
	1050	104	142	36.5	128	172	34.4			
	1100	74	108	45.9	98	128	30.6			
Commercial Union	160	14½	26	79.3	20	29	45.0	168	170	1.2
	180	7	9	28.6	11	12	9.1			
Consol. Gold.	180	42	75	78.6	48	78	62.5	211	248	17.5
	200	27	55	103.7	35	58	65.7			
	220	18	35	94.4	23	46	100			
Courtaulds	100	18½	12	(29.7)	20	15	(25.0)	113	107	(5.3)
	110	11	7½	(31.8)	13½	9½	(29.6)			
	120	6	4½	(25.0)	9	6½	(27.8)			
	130	4	—	(100.0)	—	—	—			
GEC	330	66	124	87.9	76	142	86.8	382	435	13.9
	360	45	97	115.6	56	115	105.4			
	390	26	71	173.1	38	89	134.2			
Grand Metropolitan	100	45½	68	49.5	47½	70	47.4	140	162	15.7
	110	36	58	61.1	38	60	57.9			
	120	27	48	77.8	29½	50	69.5			
	130	19	38	100	22	40	81.8			
	140	13	29	123.1	18½	32	73.0			

(Table continued)

Table 10.2. *(Continued)*

Share	Ex price	May option price		Percentage gain (loss)	August option price		Percentage gain (loss)	November option price		Percentage gain (loss)
		9 Mar. 79	11 May 79		9 Mar. 79	11 May 79		9 Mar. 79	11 May 79	
Boots	180	42	46	9.5	45	—	—	51	—	—
	200	24	26	8.3	29	33	13.8	36	42	16.7
	220	11½	9	(13.0)	17½	19	8.6	25	28	12.0
	240	4	2	(50.0)	—	10		—	19	
	260	2	1	(50.0)	—	—		—	—	

Share price 215 (9 Mar. 79), 224 (11 May 79) = 4.2% gain

Share	Ex price	May option price		Percentage gain (loss)	August option price		Percentage gain (loss)	November option price		Percentage gain (loss)
EMI	110	18	6	(66.7)	22	12	(45.5)	26	16	(38.5)
	120	11	3	(72.7)	16	8	(50.0)	21	12	(42.9)
	130	7	1	(85.7)	11	6	(45.5)	16	10	(37.5)
	140	4	¼	(93.8)	8	4½	(43.8)	12	9	(25.0)

Share price 120 (9 Mar. 79), 105 (11 May 79) = (12.5%) loss

Share	Ex price	May option price		Percentage gain (loss)	August option price		Percentage gain (loss)	November option price		Percentage gain (loss)
Imperial Group	80	22½	23½	4.4	25	27	8.0	26½	29½	11.3
	90	13½	14½	7.7	15½	18½	19.4	17	21	23.5
	100	7	4½	(35.7)	8½	9	5.9	10½	12	12.5

Share price 100 (9 Mar. 79), 101.5 (11 May 79) = (12.5%) loss

Share	Ex price	May option price		Percentage gain (loss)	August option price		Percentage gain (loss)	November option price		Percentage gain (loss)
RTZ	260	57	—	—	62	95	53.2	—	—	—
	280	39	54	38.5	49	78	59.2	58	99	70.7
	300	24	34	41.7	38	62	63.2	46	84	82.6

Share price 308 (9 Mar. 79), 332 (11 May 79) = 7.8% gain.

Share	Ex price	July option price			October option price			Share price		
		9 Mar. 79	11 May 79	Percentage gain (loss)	9 Mar. 79	11 May 79	Percentage gain	9 Mar. 79	11 May 79	Percentage gain (loss)
ICI	330	89	78	(12.4)	94	85	(9.6)	404	396	(2.0)
	360	61	48	(21.3)	65	58	(10.8)			
	390	37	26	(29.7)	45	37	(17.8)			
	420	18½	12	(29.7)	25	20	(20.0)			
Land Securities	240	57	78	36.8	65	88	35.4	287	308	7.3
	260	41	58	41.5	48	69	43.8			
	280	26	41	57.7	34	53	55.9			
	300	15	25	66.7	23	42	82.6			
Marks & Spencer	80	26	47	80.8	28	50	78.6	101	123	21.8
	90	17	37	117.6	19	40	110.5			
	100	10½	27	157.1	12	30	150.0			
Shell Transport	550	165	243	47.3	170	—	65.6	698	764	9.5
	600	115	193	67.8	125	207	70.7			
	650	75	143	90.7	92	157	111.3			
	700	43	95	120.9	53	112				

Share	Ex price	May option price			August option price			November option price		
		9 Mar. 79	11 May 79	Percentage gain (loss)	9 Mar. 79	11 May 79	Percentage gain	9 Mar. 79	11 May 79	Percentage gain (loss)
BOC	60	17½	20½	17.1	18½	24	29.7	—	—	—
	70	8½	11	29.4	9½	15½	63.2	11	20	81.8
	80	2	2½	25.0	5	9	80	7	11½	64.3

Share price 75 (9 Mar. 79), 79½ (11 May 79) = 6.0% gain

ately, we cannot go through the same exercise of computing gains at a subsequent market peak because there has been no obvious peak between August 1984 and the time of writing. In order to get some appreciation of the behaviour of shares and options since August 1984, we can take an arbitrary point, say nearly at the end of the year, on 21st December 1984. The share prices and the appropriate option prices are given in the Table for both 4th August and 21st December 1984, so allowing a comparison of the two as for the 1979 market. In this case the best performer was Hanson, whose price moved from 146 to 310, for a gain of 112.33% during the period. Because of the longer time-scale between the buying point and this valuation point, only one option series was available to cover the period— the March 220's—which gained 675%.

The worst performing share during the period was De Beers, which showed a loss of −36.17%. Five option series spanned the 4-month period from August to December: the January 180's, losing 76.9%, the January 200s, losing 84.6%, the January 220s, losing 91.6%, the April 200's, losing 75% and the April 220s, losing 76.1%. The average loss for these five series was 80.8%, about eight times the loss in the share price.

Of course, losses such as these only become meaningful if we have no way of selecting in advance those shares which are going to be successful and those which are not when the market starts to climb. We have already formulated a successful selection procedure when we are given a choice of all the shares available on the market. Remember our criteria were high volatility and strength in a falling market. When we chose our list in Chapter 6, we used the volatility, in terms of the ratio of the 1978/9 high to the 1978/9 low as at 12th January 1979, during the falling market. We then calculated the strength of the shares by seeing how far they had risen or fallen from their previous peak (the 1978/9 high) on 9th March 1979, when the buying signal was given. If we carry out the same operations on the 15 shares in the traded options market, we get the data given in Table 10.4. What we are trying to get from these data is a correlation between the gains and losses in the share price between 9th March 1979 and 11th May 1979 and the figures for volatility and strength. One obvious point that is pleasing is that the worst performing share, EMI, with a 12.5% loss, is also the weakest, with a strength of 63.2%, i.e. its price at 9th March 1979 was only 63.2% of its previous peak in 1977/8, so naturally we would not have bought options in such a share.

Table 10.4 shows that the average volatility, in terms of the ratio of the 1977/8 high/low values, was 1.33 or better. This procedure gives the six shares shown in Table 10.5.

The results show that this is a good method of selection, since the average gain in the share price of this group of six was 12.95%, just about double the gain in the original list of 15 shares. Not only that, but the procedure

Table 10.3. Share prices and offer prices on 4 Aug. 84 and 21 Dec. 84 on various series in the traded options market

Ex price	Jan. option price 4 Aug. 84	Jan. option price 21 Dec. 84	Percentage gain	Apr. option price 4 Aug. 84	Apr. option price 21 Dec. 84	Percentage gain	Share price 4 Aug. 84	Share price 21 Dec. 84	Percentage gain (loss)
British Petroleum									
420	37	52	40.54	45	60	33.33	455	465	. 2.20
460	20	25	25.00	27	25	− 7.41			
500	9	7	− 22.22						
550	5	3	− 40.00						
Consol. Gold.									
460	57	35	− 38.60	65	47	− 27.69	510	483	− 5.29
500	37	14	− 62.16	45	28	− 37.78			
550	24	4	− 83.33						
600	12	1	− 91.67						
650	7	1	− 85.71						
Courtaulds									
110	15	17	13.33	18	19	5.56	120	126	5.00
120	8	8.5	6.25	13	11	− 15.38			
130	6	3.5	− 41.67						
140	4	1.5	− 62.50						
160	2	1	− 50.00						
Commercial Union									
180	39	9	− 76.92	32	8	− 75.00	208	182	− 12.50
200	26	4	− 84.62	21	5	− 76.19			
220	18	1.5	− 91.67						
GEC									
160	36	58	61.11	40	62	55.00	206	214	3.88
180	20	38	90.00	26	42	61.54			
200	9	22	144.44	15	28	86.67			
Grand Metropolitan									
280	28	27	− 3.57	36	35	− 2.78	302	302	0.00
300	18	12	− 33.33	24	22	− 8.33			
330	8	3	− 62.50						
360	3	1	− 66.67						

(Table continued)

Table 10.3.(Continued)

		Jan. option price			Apr. option price			Share price		
	Ex price	4 Aug 84	21 Dec.84	Percentage gain	4 Aug. 84	21 Dec. 84	Percentage gain	4 Aug. 84	21 Dec. 84	Percentage gain (loss)
ICI	550	28	196	600.00	40	202	405.00	586	742	26.62
	600	12	146	1116.67						
	650	7	96	1271.43						
Land Securities	260	30	53	76.67	36	57		287	310	8.01
	280	17	34	100.00	21	39				
	300	9	16	77.78						
Marks & Spencer	100	29	18	−37.93				120	115	−4.17
	110	18	10	−44.44						
	120	8	4	−50.00						
	130	4	1.75	−68.75						
Shell Transport	550	37	87	135.14	45	95		590	630	6.78
	600	22	43	95.45	27	55				
	650	12	13	8.33						
	700	6	3	−50.00						
		Feb. option price								
Barclays	420	55	142	158.18				450	554	23.11
	460	30	102	240.00						
	500	17	62	264.71						
Imperial Group	140	16	40	150.00				146	175	19.86
	160	9	21	133.33						
	180	3	7	133.33						
LASMO	280	27	42	55.56				280	312	11.43
	300	18	27	50.00						
	330	12	18	50.00						

	Strike		March option price				
Lonrho	130	18	34	88.89	146	161	10.27
	140	11	24	118.18			
	160	6	10	66.67			
P & O	280	42	27	−35.71	303	302	−.33
	300	29	13	−55.17			
	330	17	5	−70.59			
Racal	200	42	64	52.38	235	256	8.94
	220	26	44	69.23			
	240	16	27	68.75			
RTZ	500	62	97	56.45	577	583	1.04
	550	42	47	11.90			
	600	22	25	13.64			
	650	13	6.5	−50.00			
Vaal Reefs	90	13	5	−61.54	78	72	−7.69
	100	9.5	2.5	−73.68			
Beecham	300	25	92	268.00	350	385	10.00
	330	11	62	463.64			
Bass	390	15	85	466.67	380	468	23.16
De Beers	550	58	7	−87.93	564	360	−36.17
GKN	140	35	54	54.29	167	190	13.77
	160	19	34	78.95			
	180	10	18	80.00			
Hanson	220	12	93	675.00	146	310	112.33
Tesco	180	9	55	511.11	174	231	32.76

pulled in the best performance of the bunch, Marks & Spencer, and four out of the top five shares in the list. That is not bad by any standards, especially considering that we have operated purely on prices, without reading any news about the various companies' performance in terms of turnover, profits, takeover bids or any of the other information so dear to the hearts of the fundamentalists.

If we had bought the best performing options series in each of these six shares, we would have made an average gain of 110.7%, about eight and a half times that in the actual series themselves. More realistically, by taking an average of all the available series in the shares, the gain would have been 75.5%, about six times the gain in the share themselves.

The relationship between share prices and option prices can be seen by comparing the share price of Marks & Spencer and the prices of the October 80 and October 90 series from 26th January, 1979 onwards as shown in Figure 10.1. We can see that the share price made approximately a 50% gain from this point by 4th May, the peak of the share price. The October 80s made a 330% gain and the October 90s about a 225% gain. The shapes of the curves for the two series are almost identical, and have almost a constant difference of about 9p. The option prices peak out at the same time that the share price peaks out, but an interesting point is that the share price retreated about 42% from its peak, but the option prices fell back 57% from their peaks. Thus in a rising share market the option market seems to be over-optimistic, but becomes pessimistic in a falling share market.

Table 10.4. Gains and losses in share prices between 9 Mar. 1979 and 11 May 1979

Share	1978/79		Volatility high/low	Price at 9 Mar. 79	Strength as percentage of 78/79 high	Percentage gain (loss) at 11 May 79
	High	Low				
BP	954	720	1.33	1112.5	116.6	11.2
Comm. Union	164	132	1.24	168	102.4	1.2
Consol. Gold.	204	163	1.25	211	103.4	17.5
Courtaulds	131	109	1.20	113	86.3	(5.3)
GEC	349	233	1.50	382	109.5	13.9
Grand Met.	121	87	1.39	140	115.7	15.7
ICI	421	328	1.28	404	96.0	(2.0)
Land Secs	253	190	1.33	287	113.4	7.3
M & S	94	67.5	1.39	101	107.4	21.8
Shell	602	484	1.24	698	115.9	9.5
BOC	79	63	1.25	75	94.9	6.0
Boots	237	184	1.29	215	90.7	4.2
EMI	190	130	1.46	120	63.2	(12.5)
Imperial	89	71.5	1.24	100	112.4	1.5
RTZ	263	164	1.60	308	117.1	7.8
Averages			1.33		103.0	6.52

Table 10.5. Shares from the traded options list which have above average volatility and strength

Share	Percentage gain in share price, 9 Mar.–11 May 1979	Percentage gain in best option	Average percentage gain for all option series
BP	11.2	45.9	34.8
GEC	13.9	173.1	117.2
Grand Met.	15.7	123.1	74.1
Land Securities	7.3	82.6	52.6
Marks & Spencer	21.8	157.1	115.8
Rio Tinto Zinc	7.8	82.6	58.4
Average	12.95	110.7	75.5

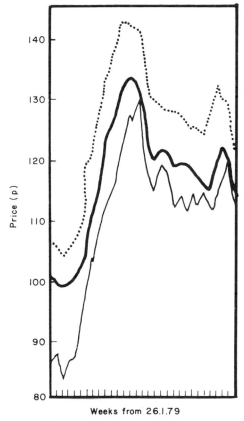

Weeks from 26.1.79

Figure 10.1. Traded options: light line, share price of Marks & Spencer; heavy line, the price of the October 90s option with 90p added; broken line, the price of the October 80s option with 90p added (90p is added instead of 80p in order to avoid overlap with the 90s option trace).

So far we have only discussed the gains which would have been made in these option series by using the 13-week moving average of the FT Index to generate a buying signal. This signal is of course one which we have recommended for the 'cautious' investor to use. Now it is debatable whether the adjective 'cautious' can be applied to those who use the traded options market. It is probably more appropriate that investors in the traded options market be described as 'aggressive', so that they should use the 5-week moving average. As far as early 1979 is concerned, the 5-week moving average of the FT index turned up a week earlier than the 13-week one, on 2nd March. Buying at this time would have resulted in much cheaper prices, both for the shares themselves, and for the various option series. The gains which would have resulted from investment on 2nd March 1979 in the six companies which we chose earlier on the grounds of volatility and strength are shown in Table 10.6, which should be compared directly with Table 10.5.

The extra week gained at the beginning of the rise in the market resulted in a gain of about 50% on the average gains for the share prices, best option prices and the average for all the option series. The same comment applies here, though, as for shares as far as the 5-week moving average is concerned. It will lead to greater profits on those occasions when it correctly foretells a prolonged upturn in the market, but often it can be wrong, thus introducing a greater element of risk. It is simply a matter of personal preference as to whether you are prepared to take greater risk in order to give yourself the potential for a larger profit.

The method of testing a group of six shares based on volatility and strength can now be applied to the 1984 market. Unfortunately, as has been pointed out previously, there has been no obvious market peak since then, so any conclusions drawn from the position in December 1984 may not be very relevant. Table 10.7 shows the volatility and gains and losses in the shares available in the 1984 traded options market. The average volatility

Table 10.6. Shares from the traded options list which have above average volatility and strength

Share	Percentage gain in share price, 2 Mar.–11 May 1979	Percentage gain in best option	Average percentage gain for all option series
BP	19.3	129.0	106.0
GEC	21.2	212.9	172.9
Grand Met.	21.3	153.3	117.0
Land Securities	9.2	86.4	61.8
Marks & Spencer	33.7	311.1	225.4
Rio Tinto Zinc	11.4	89.6	113.7
Average	19.4	163.7	132.8

Table 10.7. Gains and losses in the share prices between 4 Aug. 84 and 21 Dec. 84

Share	High	Low	Volatility High/low	Price at 4 Aug. 84	Strength	Price at 21 Dec. 84	Percentage gain (loss)
British Petroleum	518	395	1.31	455	87.84	465	2.20
Consol. Goldfields	627	487	1.29	510	81.34	483	−5.29
Courtaulds	154	120	1.28	120	77.92	126	5.00
Commercial Union	231	171	1.35	208	90.04	182	−12.50
GEC	208	174	1.20	206	99.04	214	3.88
Grand Metropolitan	352	270	1.30	302	85.80	302	.00
ICI	650	572	1.14	586	90.15	742	26.62
Land Securities	290	249	1.16	287	98.97	310	8.01
Marks & Spencer	135	106	1.27	120	88.89	115	−4.17
Shell	675	568	1.19	590	87.41	630	6.78
Barclays	575	473	1.22	450	78.26	554	23.11
Imperial	159	138	1.15	146	91.82	175	19.86
LASMO	350	275	1.27	280	80.00	312	11.43
Lonrho	150	105	1.43	146	97.33	161	10.27
P & O	325	240	1.35	303	93.23	302	−.33
Racal	229	192	1.19	235	102.62	256	8.94
RTZ	718	593	1.21	577	80.36	583	1.04
Vaal Reefs	95.88	70	1.37	78	81.35	72	−7.69
Beecham	338	291	1.16	350	103.55	385	10.00
Bass	380	300	1.27	380	100.00	468	23.16
De Beers	616	510	1.21	564	91.56	360	−36.17
GKN	218	174	1.25	167	76.61	190	13.77
Hanson	198	162.5	1.22	146	73.74	310	112.33
Tesco	196	166	1.18	174	88.78	231	32.76
Averages			1.25		88.61		10.54

Table 10.8. Share from Table 10.7 selected for volatility and strength

Share	Percentage gain in share 4 Aug. 84–21 Dec. 84	Percentage gain in best option	Average gain for all option series
British Petroleum	2.20	40.54	4.87
Commercial Union	− 12.50	− 76.00	80.88
Marks & Spencer	− 4.10	− 37.93	− 50.28
P & O	− .33	− 35.71	− 53.79
Lonrho	10.27	118.18	91.21
Bass	23.16	466.67	232.15
	3.12	79.46	50.84

is 1.25, and the average strength is 88.61%. Selecting those shares which have above this strength and above this volatility gives the list shown in Table 10.8. This list underperforms the larger group from which they have been selected, showing an average gain in the share price of 3.1%, compared with 10.5% for the whole group. This is mainly because of the inclusion of Commercial Union, which lost 12.5% by 21st December. Note that, at the time of writing, Commercial Union have come back and are now standing at a gain of about 12% on the August 1984 value. The difficulties of drawing conclusions from this selection are therefore almost entirely due to the arbitrary selection of a time-scale for the exercise.

Again, the gearing obtained by investment in options rather than the underlying securities themselves can be seen by the gains in the Bass options—466.6%, compared with the share price gain of 23.1%, and the losses in the Commercial Union options—75.0% compared with the loss in the share price of 12.5%.

An interesting way to picture the market's thinking about the share price during its rise and fall is to add the striking price and the contract price. This value gives an idea of what the market thinks the share price will reach in the weeks ahead before the series expires. In this context the market means the balance point between those buying options, who think the market will rise, and those writing options, who think the market will fall. In Figure 10.1 is plotted the actual share price of Marks & Spencer and the price of the October 90s series, with 90p added and the price of the October 80s series, also with 90p added to avoid overlap with the 90s series. Obviously, at the end of January, when the share price was 85p, the market expected it to reach 100p between then and the expiry date. By mid-April, when the share price was in the high 120s, the traded options market saw it reaching only a fraction higher, to 133p between then and October. By the end of August the market expectation was for a peak of 110p. At the beginning of the rise in February, therefore, the options market was highly optimistic, seeing a price rise of about 18% in Marks & Spencer shares, but by the end of August, when the share price was 108p, the market could see only a rise to 110p, a gain of less than 2%.

Since our whole attitude to the stock market is one of attempting to predict whether share prices are going to go up or down, we may well ask ourselves how good the traded option market is at this, since it is what the options market is all about. At the very least the options market gives us a chance to test the thinking of a fairly large body of people—those who buy and sell options—against our own personal conclusions about the short-term future of shares. So, if the prices of options are rising, but we have concluded that the market is due to fall, then this disparity needs to be checked out very carefully. This is not to say that we are necessarily wrong, since it is often the lone voice that is correct. It does mean that we have to be very sure of the facts upon which we have based our divergent opinion.

To show that this investigation of the predictive power of the traded options market may well be a fruitful area of research, it is useful to show how good the traded options market was in 1979 at predicting a share price. Conclusions to be drawn from more recent markets will require extensive statistical examination which is outside the scope of this present book, but the 1979 data are presented here as a thought-provoking exercise.

Hitherto, we have only been able to draw conclusions about two properties of share prices—firstly that they have started to rise, and secondly that they have started to fall. Both of these occurrences tend to happen rather suddenly, so that we have virtually no warning that the market has taken off, but rely on moving averages confirming that the rise has started some weeks after the event. The same thing happens when the market tops out; it is not until the peak has passed that the moving averages or other indicators that we have discussed in Chapter 7 tell us what has happened. Another unsatisfactory point is that, once we are certain that the market is headed upwards, we have only the haziest idea of how high the shares will rise, although we can get some information by the methods discussed in Chapter 11. Even when the trend upwards has been under way for some time, we have no information that would enable us to update our prediction as to the highest price that will be reached.

However, the traded options market does exactly that: the market is continually updating its view of what the peak price will be. Because of this aspect, we can look at the options market in Marks & Spencer shares, as just one example, in a new light; namely, how good is the market in predicting the peak price of Marks & Spencer shares? The difficulty is in deciding how to score such predictions. It is easy to say that if a price of 130p is predicted, and that is the exact peak that the market reaches, then the market is 100% right, but what is the prediction that would make the market 100% wrong? Would it be a value of zero, a price which stays the

Table 10.9. 1979 Marks & Spencer share prices and prices predicted by the October 90 series traded options

Date	Share price	Traded options predicted price	Predicted peak as percentage of actual peak
26 Jan. 79	85	100	74.6
2 Feb. 79	87	99	73.9
9 Feb. 79	82	97½	72.8
16 Feb. 79	86	99	73.9
23 Feb. 79	86	99	73.9
2 Mar. 79	92	102	76.1
9 Mar. 79	103	109	81.3
16 Mar. 79	102	110	82.1
23 Mar. 79	109	117	87.3
30 Mar. 79	112	123	91.8
6 Apr. 79	114	125	93.3
13 Apr. 79	120	130	97.0
20 Apr. 79	127	132	98.5
27 Apr. 79	125	133	99.3
4 May 79	130	131	97.8
11 May 79	123	130	97.0

same, or simply a fall in price instead of a rise? For our purposes we can adopt a system in which we express the predicted price as a percentage of the actual peak reached, which during the week ended 11th May 1979 was 134p. The data are given in Table 10.9; the figures are impressive, since they showed that the options market, 2 weeks before the peak price was reached, was able to predict that price to within 99.3%, or 1p, of the actual peak. Even 1 month before the peak the traded options market was 93.3% correct, predicting a high of 125p against the actual value of 134p.

Thus the traded options market gives us another tool in our quest for a better prediction of what the stock market is about to do. We should pay a great deal of attention to what this mini-market is saying, even if we do not intend to buy or sell options.

Chapter 11

Moving Averages as Predictors of Share Price Movements

So far in this book we have utilized moving averages as predictors of share price movements only in the simplest sense that when these averages turn up, after falling for some time, then we can predict a general rise for some months ahead. Although we can never be absolutely certain that such a rise will occur, the odds are greatly in favour of it because of the past behaviour of the market. In this chapter we are going to look more closely at individual share price, with a view to deciding whether moving averages can be used to predict a price range into which the share prices will move in the near future. Naturally, the odds against being able to predict a *price* for a share rather than just the *direction* of price movement must be considerably less in our favour. However, it should become clear that there is much to be gained in this area from a closer study of moving averages.

We have already shown a chart of the 13-week moving averages of a number of shares, and one of these will serve again to illustrate a number of points. In the chart for Babcock shown in Fig. 11.1 are drawn 13-week and 103-week moving averages, as well as the weekly closing prices, for the period 1970 to mid-1980. A close study of both of these charts will give rise to two observations, from which we may draw further conclusions later in this chapter.

1. The longer the averaging period, the smoother the resulting curve. Because of the mathematics of moving averages, the longer the period of time we use for averaging, the smoother will be the plot of the resulting averages. It would take several weeks or perhaps months of collapse of a share price before the 103-week (2-year) moving average will start to turn down. Because of the way in which averages are

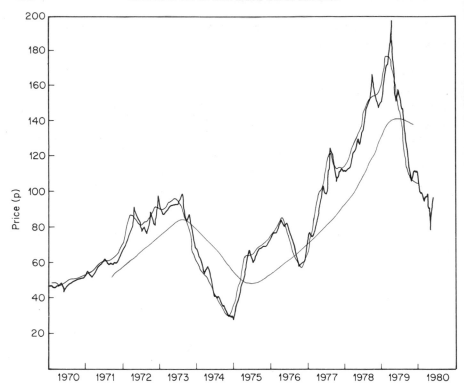

Figure 11.1. Price movements of the shares of Babcock since 1970. The 13-week moving average is shown in red and the 103-week moving average is in green.

calculated, the value for the average should be placed half a span behind in time. Thus the 103-week average is plotted 1 year behind the present time. Although the peak price of 198p was reached in May 1979, it took another 30 weeks or so until the 103-week average topped out. On the other hand, the 13-week average, being much more responsive to a sustained fall in prices, was seen to turn down only a few weeks after the peak price was attained. The penalty for this extra smoothness attainable in a moving average is, of course, that the delay is so long before it reverses direction that it is entirely useless as a buying or selling signal. For example, by the time the 103-week average topped out, some 30 weeks after the peak price, the share price had fallen to around 110p, giving an unacceptable loss. On the other hand, the advantage of the smooth curve is that it is much easier to extrapolate by eye into the future, and it is this aspect which is so important in predicting future price ranges.

2. We can draw sensible limits for the extent to which prices move away from moving averages.

Figure 11.1 shows that the weekly closing prices of a share meanders about the 13-week average and the 103-week average, while the 13-week average also meanders around the 103-week average. We can draw reasonable limits for the extent to which prices move away from the 103-week average. The further away the price moves from this average, the greater is the likelihood that it will reverse direction and return to the moving average. This is easily demonstrated by looking at the differences between the share price and the 103-week moving average every week from the start of this average to its last point on the chart in Fig. 11.1. These are expressed as a percentage of the moving average value, ignoring the positive or negative nature of the difference, in the histogram shown in Fig. 11.2. This shows that for 54.1% of the time the price was less than 10% away from the moving average, and for 79.0% of the time the price was less than 20% away from the moving average. This means that we can construct a band by drawing a line, following the 103-week average and 20% of its value higher, and a second line 20% of its value lower. The price then stayed within this band 79% of the time. Of course, the figures will vary somewhat from one share to another, since they will have different short-term volatilities. The figures will also vary slightly if different time-scales are employed for the same share. For example, between 1980 and early 1985, the Babcock price stayed within the 20% band 75% of the time. By combining these two features of ease of extrapolation and a limit where the chances are 80:20 that the price will not penetrate the limit, we can begin to

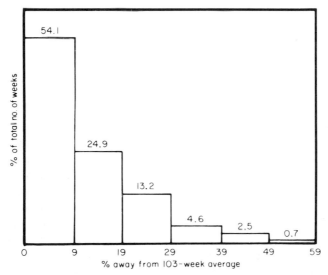

Figure 11.2. A histogram of the number of weeks the price of Babcock shares spent at certain percentages away from the 103-week moving average.

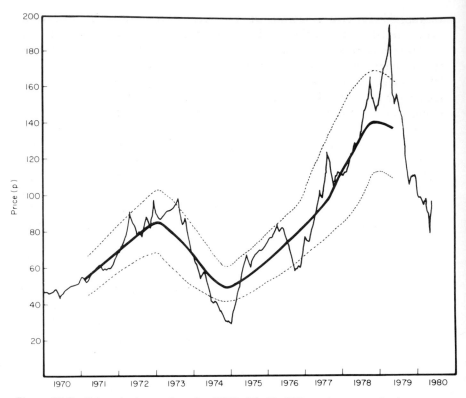

Figure 11.3. Babcock share prices for 1970–80. Th 103-week average is shown as a solid heavy line. The dotted lines above and below the average represent the limits of 20% price movements away from the average.

formulate a method of using moving averages as an aid to prediction of prices.

In Fig. 11.3 the weekly closing prices for Babcock and the 103-week moving average are plotted. Superimposed on this are the two limit lines, above and below this moving average, representing price movements of ± 20% from the moving average. The main disadvantage in using this chart to test what decisions we might have made at various periods since 1970, utilizing the concepts we have developed, is that we have the benefit of hindsight. We can see that there were reversals of the 103-week moving average in early 1973, early 1975 and early 1979. Of course, at those dates we would not have known that, since the averages would have been lagging behind by 1 year, for the reasons outlined earlier. A good exercise here to help with decision-making is to cover with a sheet of paper all that chart to the right of a specified time in which we are interested. At that particular time we also need to erase mentally the moving average and limit lines for a whole year backwards in time. If we suppose that we did the exercise for somewhere in the beginning of 1973, we would see the situation as drawn in Fig. 11.4. There is obviously, at that point, nothing to tell us that the 103-week moving average will be turning down sharply in a year's time, although it is curving slightly, the slope decreasing constantly. Our efforts at extrapolation would produce the dotted lines shown in Fig. 11.4, and we could see that the price is near the predicted 103-week average, and not at either of the extremes. At such a point we are in neither a buy nor a sell situation, and in any case a glance at the chart as it would have been a couple of months earlier shows that we would have sold then. This is because we would have been out towards the upper limit which we would have been predicting to be about 100p. At such a point the chances are about 80:20 that the price will retreat towards the value of the average itself. Caution would dictate that we wait for the price to retreat slightly, in order to cover for the 20% chance that the price will rise even further.

To return to the present point, we are presented with two possibilities; either the price will rise again from its value near the average towards the upper limit which will be somewhere between 105 and 110p, or it will fall

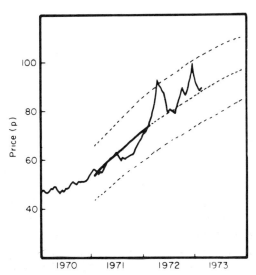

Figure 11.4. Babcock share prices for 1970–73. The 103-week average is shown, along with its projection into the future. The 20% price limits above and below the average are shown as dotted lines.

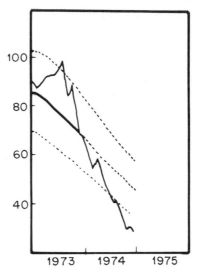

Figure 11.5. Babcock share prices for 1973–75. The 103-week average is shown, along with its projection into the future. The 20% limits above and below the average are shown as dotted lines.

towards the lower limit which is around 80p. In fact the price rose to just below 100p, but then suffered a sustained fall for over a year.

Another point of interest on the chart in Fig. 11.3 is that at the end of 1974 and beginning of 1975. The situation as we would have been plotting it at the time appears in Fig. 11.5. Once again, we would not be able to predict the upturn that then transpired in the 103-week moving average, and this upturn would not have become obvious until a year later. We would almost certainly have extrapolated the moving average and the upper and lower limits as shown in Fig. 11.5. By doing this we would see that the actual share price is somewhere near the predicted lower limit of 30p. We would therefore have been starting to think of this as a buying opportunity, since the chances are much more in favour of a rise back towards the moving average than for a further fall. We would of course wait for a positive sign that such a rise was under way by watching for a slight rise back from the present position. By doing this we would have bought in at around 35p, and would have sold in mid-1975 at around 68p for a very useful profit. You may ask why we would have sold at this point, since the chart in Fig. 11.3 shows the 103-week average rising strongly, with very much further to go. The reason is that, at that time in mid-1975, we had no firm indication that the 103-week average had turned up from its downward trend. We might have expected a turn-up, since the share price of 68p was so far out of line from a predicted price of about 40p that this must eventually work its way into the average, but on the other hand this high price may well have turned out to be a temporary peak. However, the first sign of a retreat from this high point would have been an indication to sell, since the odds were against a further upward trend in the short term.

Between 1975 and 1979 there were two more trading opportunities signalled by the moving average, in late 1976 and late 1977. A predicted 103-week moving average, and the upper and lower limits for this period, are shown in Fig. 11.6. Towards the end of 1976 the price had fallen below the boundary of the extrapolated lower limit. A rise towards the average then signalled a good buying opportunity at about 65p. Depending on the slope of this upward trend, the price could be expected to move into a range somewhere between 100p and 120p. With a hiccup at 100p, which presumably forms some kind of psychological barrier (note earlier unsuccessful attempts to rise above this) the price reached the predicted upper limit in late 1977, and then retreated back towards the average. Thus a gain of nearly 100% could have been made by buying and selling operations based on these predictions.

A significant feature of Fig. 11.3 is of course the peak price briefly attained in May 1979, which was followed by a rapid collapse in price. This

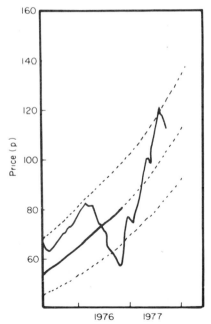

Figure 11.6. Babcock share prices for 1976–77. THe 103-week average is shown, along with its projection into the future. The 20% limits above and below the average are shown as dotted lines.

is a critical test for the value of predictions based on moving averages, since a wrong decision at this point in time would have led to a catastrophic halving of the value of an investment in Babcock over the following year.

An inspection of Fig. 11.7, which shows how the position would have looked in May 1979, indicates that the price of 198p was about touching the upper limit which would be obtained by extrapolation of the 103-week average and its limits. Hence the chances of a further rise at that point are 80:20 against, and a slight retreat in price should have been taken as an indicator to sell. We would have been able to come out from Babcock at somewhere around 190p, so that we can say without qualification that an analysis of the 103-week moving average and the limits within which the price spends about 80% of its time were successful in preserving the capital gain made by previous successful buying operations.

Figure 11.3 is identical with that presented in the first edition of this book. The prediction was made then (May 1980) that because the price of 90p was towards the lower limit of the 20% boundary, then once it moved back towards the average, a rise towards the 110–120p price band could be expected. Figure 11.8 shows a chart, produced by microcomputer, of the

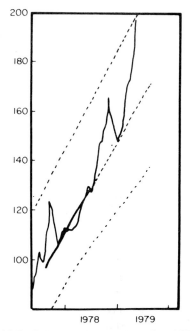

Figure 11.7. Babcock share prices for 1978–79. The 103-week average is shown, along with its projection into the future. The 20% limits above and below the average are shown as dotted lines.

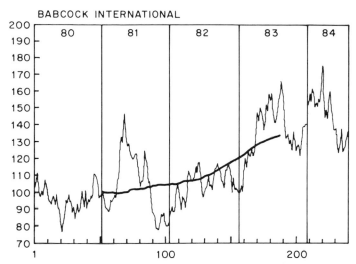

Figure 11.8. Microcomputer plot of the Babcock share price and 103-week average (heavy line) from 1980 to mid-1984.

Babcock price, and the 103-week moving average from 1980 to mid-1984. This enables us to test the prediction made in the first edition. The price did not begin to move towards the moving average until August 1980, and then, as predicted, moved up to 110p, although it did not reach 120p.

The sharp spike in 1981 exceeded the projected 20% boundary comfortably, and again, the investor would have been extremely watchful once the 120p mark was exceeded. Once sold, somewhere in May 1981, the investor would have been waiting for the next buying opportunity once the price dropped about 20p below the projected average line of around the 100p mark. Surely enough, this occurred later in the year in November, and the price made a reasonable gain, after a few minor hiccups, to above 110p. The reader may judge for himself the efficiency of this method of price projection for the buying point at the end of 1982, and selling point somewhere in mid-1983, and the not so clear-cut buying point in late 1983, but clear selling point in March 1984.

In order to study the more recent behaviour of the share price of Babcock, an expanded chart is shown from June 1983 to the present time (May 1985) in Fig. 11.9. It can be seen by close inspection that the 103-week average superimposed on the chart, and terminating about the end of March 1984 (because it is lagging 1 year behind the present time), has begun to flatten out. This suggests that the projected average will curve slightly downwards. The implication for the price of Babcock through 1985 is therefore an oscillation between a high point of about 155−160p and a low point of 110−115p.

Figure 11.9. Microcomputer plot of the Babcock share price and 103-week average (heavy line) from mid-1983 to early 1985.

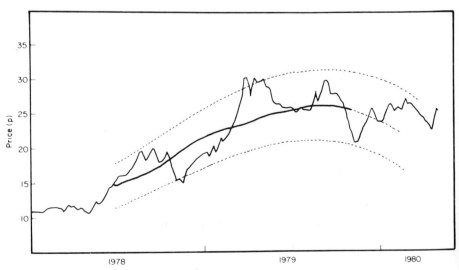

Figure 11.10. Share prices for Energy Services and Electronics 1978–80. The 51-week average is shown, along with its projection into the future. The 20% limits above and below the average are shown as dotted lines.

So far we have been utilizing an average which has a fairly long span—103-weeks being of course the nearest odd number of weeks to 2 years. However, a shorter span, say 1 year, can also give useful results, since it should be, in most cases, a reasonably smooth plot, capable of good extrapolation. An example of this is shown in Fig. 11.10, where the weekly closing prices of Energy Services and a 51-week moving average, are plotted between 1978 and 1980. A calculation shows that in this case for 85% of the time the weekly prices are within 20% of the moving average, as shown in Fig. 11.11.

The upper and lower limits of this 20% movement are shown in Fig. 11.10. We can say that when the price has reached one of these limits, there is an 85:15 chance that the price will tend to return to the average. We can carry out a predictive procedure similar to that employed for Babcock, and

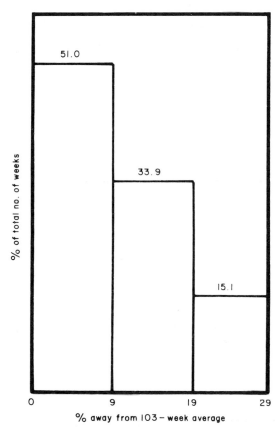

Figure 11.11. A histogram of the number of weeks the price of Energy Services and Electronics spent at certain percentages away from the 51-week moving average.

cover up the chart to the right of the point of interest, bearing in mind that the last value we would have for the 51-week average would be 26 weeks (half a span) back in time. By doing this we would find a buying situation in November 1978 as the price rebounded from a slight penetration of the lower limit. The selling situation occurred in March 1979 as the price fell back through the upper limit. The next buying time was in November 1979 when the price rose from its brief contact with the lower limit at about 21p. The shares should have been sold in March 1980 when the price came near to the extrapolated upper limit of 27.5p. Although the price fell from that point, it did not even penetrate the 51-week average, and so did not generate a buying signal by the time the right-hand side of the chart was reached.

Although it is difficult to generalize, it is unlikely that a moving average with a span less than 1 year (51 weeks to the nearest odd number; an odd number is necessary otherwise the result would have to be plotted halfway through a week) will give good results. A choice between 51 weeks and any other larger value such as 103 weeks (2-year span) will depend upon the time interval between important highs and lows in the chart of the share price. It will also depend upon how much historical data you have collected upon which to carry out such calculations. Thus 2 years of history are required to produce just the first point of the average if the 103-week average is used, and so if only a 2-year span data is available then obviously a 51-week average will yield 52 calculated points, giving a reasonable length of line upon which to base an extrapolation into the future. For the mathematically minded we can describe in more detail how a decision can be made upon the span of the average in those cases where enough data is available to cover a reasonable time span.

First of all we may ask why moving averages are of use at all in predicting price movements. The answer lies in the fact that they act as filters, although not as good as others which we can design to do the job. The better filters, however, require very much more calculation, and are therefore suitable only where a microcomputer is available to reduce the possibility of error and to take the tedium out of the process. If we are reasonably happy that share prices have ups and downs which are not totally random, but exhibit a number of periodicities that may be complex, but capable of resolution, then such filters can be used to resolve these periodicities. If we feel that a share price exhibits fluctuations that indicate fairly dominant components of say 31- and 51-week periodicity, then a 31-week moving average will filter out the component of 31-week periodicity and highlight the 51-week component. A 51-week moving average will remove the 51-week component and highlight components of even longer duration. Because these filters are not perfect, we will still see traces of higher frequencies come through, although they will be out of phase. For example, with the 51-week moving average there could still be a proportion

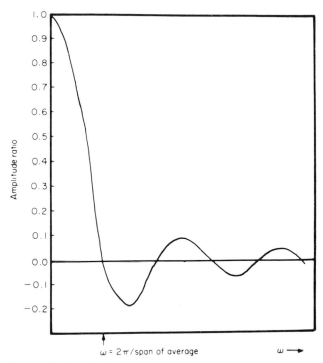

Figure 11.12. The frequency response of a moving average.

of the 31-week component apparent in the average, although it will be attenuated compared with the original before applying the average.

An idea of the frequency response of a moving average can be gained from Fig. 11.12, where amplitude ratio is plotted against $\omega = \pi/t$, (where t = time). In this figure the frequency is increasing as we go from left to right. The figure shows that a cut-off point occurs where $\omega = 2\pi/$(span of the average). An amplitude ratio of 1 means that that frequency is passed with no attenuation, whereas an amplitude ratio of 0 means that there is a complete cut-off for that frequency. We can see from the figure that frequencies lower than the cut-off point come through attenuated, with such attenuation getting less as the frequency gets lower. For example, a 51-week average would cause components with say a 55-week periodicity to be almost cut off, those with 103-week periodicity to be phased out considerably diminished, and those with say 401-weeks periodicity to be hardly affected. On the other hand, slightly higher frequencies, say of 41-week periodicity, would come through sharply attenuated and 180 degrees out of phase, i.e. apparently inverted. At even higher frequencies the responses are even more diminished, but come back into phase again. At higher frequencies again the output moves out of phase, and at even higher frequencies back

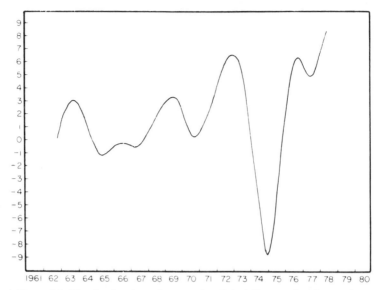

Figure 11.13. Application of a superior digital filter to the share prices of Babcock. The response is based on a 199-point weighted filter, covering the period from 1961 to 1980.

into phase. Of course, the highest frequencies we are interested in, since we are taking weekly closing prices, are for a value equivalent to 1 week, i.e. $\omega = 2\pi/1$, $\omega = 6.28$.

The only variable we have to help us in deciding on a moving average is the length of the span of the filter. There are other more superior digital filters available which rely upon weighted values with which to multiply the share prices over the span of the filter. A great deal of effort is needed in the first place to calculate the weights, which usually involve sines and cosines. Unlike the moving average calculations, which simply require the addition of the data points over the span of the average, finally dividing by the number of points in the span in order to get the first point of the moving average, filter calculations will require you to multiply each data point by its appropriate weight value before adding the lot and dividing by the number of points. As you may imagine, the scope for error and the fatigue factor are high, and this type of calculation is best suited to a microcomputer. Software to carry out such calculations is available comercially (see Appendix E) and the increasing storage capacity of the latest systems enables a great deal of stock market historical data to be maintained for this type of calculation. Figure 11.13 shows the results of applying a 19-point weighted filter to the share price of Babcock from 1961 to 1980.

Appendix A

Chart Patterns

The charting of the price movements of a share over a long period of time can be of great value in aiding investment decisions, for both buying and selling operations as we have seen with moving averages. Chartists also maintain that certain patterns repeat themselves from time to time, not only in the charts of one particular share, but in those of other shares as well. Thus they argue that if one sees a pattern emerging, it is a reasonable bet that the trend will continue in the same way that it has done on previous occasions, and a decision can be based on this. There is something to be said for this view, as can be confirmed by studying charts of several shares, going back, say, 10 years. However, for our purposes it is best not to follow patterns too slavishly, but to read them in conjunction with the other signals which we are receiving. If the chart patterns confirm the feeling we have from studying moving averages and 9-week lows etc., then we can proceed with even more confidence. If, however, the various signals are conflicting with each other, then, in the case of buying, it would perhaps be wiser to find some other share for which all the indications are positive. In a selling situation it may pay to wait a little longer until the situation has clarified. What one must not do is base our decisions entirely on patterns.

In the following pages are described some of the most common patterns, and their implication for buying and selling. Of necessity a very simple view is given, and anyone wishing for more than this is advised to read carefully the many books available on technical analysis.

1. Support line (Fig. A.1(a))

This pattern is characterized by a price fall to a certain level, a reversal to a higher level, the process being repeated several times. The lower level is thus a support line, a point at which buyers appear who adjudge the share

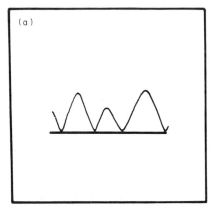
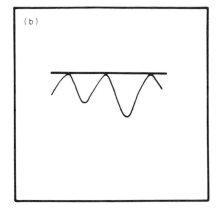

Figure A.1. (a) Support line; (b) resistance line.

to be a good buy. If we can find such a pattern on the chart, then the time to buy would be just after the price has bounced up slightly from the point where we judged the line should be drawn. We should not consider buying before this in case the support line is penetrated, i.e. it is not a support line any longer! This is discussed under heading 4. Note that we cannot expect a price to bounce up from a support line too many times. If it has already done so five or six times, say, then we should leave it alone. In common with other patterns discussed in this chapter, it is imperative to recognize them at an early stage in their formation, otherwise they can turn out to be traps for the unwary.

2. Resistance line (Fig. A.1(b))

We can regard this as the opposite of a support line. The price rises to a certain level, and then retreats before rising again back to that level. Several attempts may be made to penetrate the resistance line without success. The beginning of the fall back from this line is therefore a selling signal, indicating that the price has some way to fall. It is important to wait for a slight fall back from this line in case the line is penetrated (see heading 5).

3. Resistance becomes support (Fig. A.2)

Frequently, when a resistance line is penetrated upwards, the price eventually falls back to this line again before bouncing up again, and may repeat this action. The old resistance line has therefore become a support line. When a price pentrates a resistance line, its return back to this level should be watched carefully for the beginnings of a new upswing, since this would indicate a good buying level.

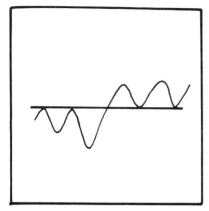

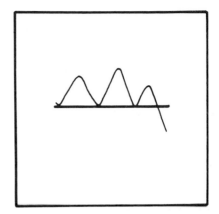

Figure A.2. Resistance lines becomes support line.

Figure A.3. Penetration of a support line.

4. Penetration of a support line (Fig. A.3)

When a share price, having returned to a resistance level several times, finally penetrates it downwards, this is considered to be bad news, and the downward fall may be expected to continue some way. Such an action on the part of a share is therefore a selling situation.

5. Penetration of a resistance line (Fig. A.4)

When the price does not retreat on rising to a previous resistance line, but continues up through it, this is considered to be an important buying signal, and the shares, if already held, should not be sold.

6. Uptrend line (Fig. A.5)

This may be considered to be a support line which is sloping upwards instead of horizontal, with the price falling to this line and bouncing back up, repeating this performance several times. A slight bounce upwards from the line is therefore taken to be a buying signal, but no action should be taken until this happens since a downward penetration of the line is a selling signal, implying a further fall in the share price.

7. Downtrend line (Fig. A.6)

This is a downwards sloping version of the resistance line. The share price tends to rise to this line and then fall back. The beginning of the fall back is a selling signal, since the share price usually retreats considerably from

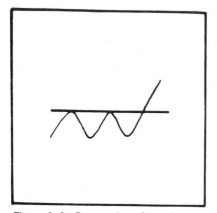

Figure A.4. Penetration of a resistance line.   **Figure A.5.** Uptrend line.

this point. However, if the share price penetrates upwards through this line, this can be considered to be a buying signal.

8. Curved uptrend line (Fig. A.7(a))

In this case the troughs of the upward waves, instead of falling on a straight line, fall onto a curve, the slope of which is beginning to flatten out. The same comments apply to this pattern as to straight uptrend lines, except that the flatter the curve becomes, the less is the possible rise from the line, and the more likely it is that the curve will turn over to become a downtrend line. The best course of action is not to use such a pattern as a buying indicator if the curve is obviously starting to flatten out, but if you have a holding in that particular share, watch closely until the curve turns downwards, and consider that to be a selling signal.

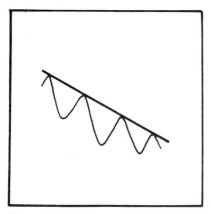

Figure A.6. Downtrend line.

9. Curved uptrend line (Fig. A.7(b))

The difference between this trendline and the previous one is that the curve line has only just started to curve upwards, and the amount of curvature is increasing. There is a greater chance that the line will continue to sweep upwards than in the case of 8, so a bounce up in the share price from this line constitutes a major buying signal.

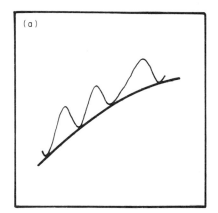
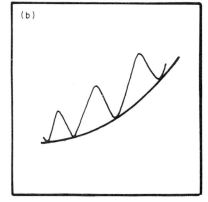

Figure A.7. Curved uptrend line: (a) curvature decreasing; (b) curvature increasing.

10. Curved downtrend lines (Fig. A.8(a) and (b))

These are curved varieties of the downtrend line 7. The peaks of the downward waves fall on a curved line instead of a straight line. As with 8 and 9, there are two versions of this, depending upon whether the curve downwards is increasing (a) or decreasing (b). If the latter, the downtrend may be coming to its end, so that a buying signal can be expected in the near future. If the curve is increasing, that is a major selling signal as soon as the share price retreats slightly from the line.

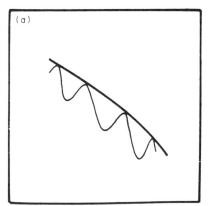
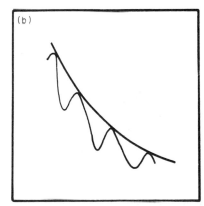

Figure A.8. Curved downtrend line: (a) curvature increasing; (b) curvature decreasing.

11. Uptrend channel (Fig. A.9)

This consists of two parallel lines, slanted upwards, between which the price yoyos. The lower line can therefore be considered to be a support line, while the upper line is a resistance line. A penetration of the lower line is a selling signal, since a further fall in price can be expected, while a penetration of the upper line is an indication of a further price rise.

12. Downtrend channel (Fig. A.10)

This consists of two parallel lines, slanted downwards, between which the price oscillates. The lower line is the support line, while the upper line is the resistance line. The same comments apply to this pattern as to the previous as far as penetration of the lines is concerned.

13. Head and shoulders (Fig. A.11)

This pattern consists of three waves, with the centre wave higher than the adjacent ones. We can draw a line through the two troughs—this is often called the 'neckline'. If the share price, after the right head wave, penetrates this neckline, this is taken to mean a further fall in price, hence such penetration is a major selling signal.

14. Double top (Fig. A.12)

The share price movement in this case is characterized by two peaks. During their formation, they might indeed be the start of the head and shoulders pattern just discussed, but the fall in price below the previous trough, which does not happen with the head and shoulders, is a signal to sell.

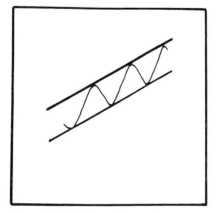

Figure A.9. Uptrend channel.

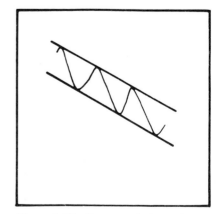

Figure A.10. Downtrend channel.

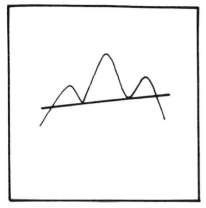

Figure A.11. Head and shoulders.

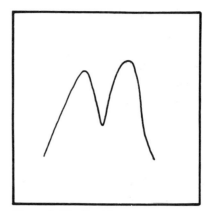

Figure A.12. Double top.

15. Spike top (Fig. A.13)

In this case the share price climbs rapidly to a peak, from which it falls just as rapidly. This is a dangerous formation, because of the usually rapid course of events. Just after the peak, it is not certain whether a double top or head and shoulders formation may be in the offing, but by the time realization sets in, a large loss could have been sustained.

16. Rounded top (Fig. A.14)

This is a much more comfortable pattern to be involved in than the previous type since the share price takes a long time to struggle over its peak. A late decision to sell in these circumstances can still result in only a limited loss of profit.

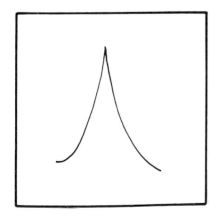

Figure A.13. Spike top.

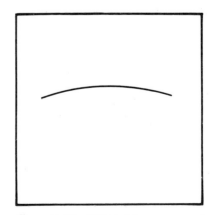

Figure A.14. Rounded top.

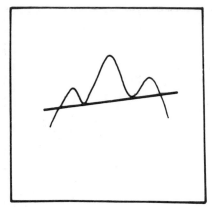

Figure A.15. Inverted head and shoulders.

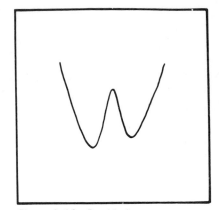

Figure A.16. Double bottom.

The bottoming patterns are really just exactly the opposite of those just discussed and, of course, the opposite comments apply, in the sense that these represent buying opportunities rather than signals to sell. The inverted head and shoulders is shown in Fig. A.15, double bottom in Fig. A.16, 'V' bottom in Fig. A.17 and saucer bottom in Fig. A.18.

The charts of share prices over a long period of time usually show several of the patterns we have been discussing. We have used John Brown shares to illustrate many aspects of this book, hence it is appropriate to point out the occurrence of many chart patterns in the 10-year period since 1970, as shown if Fig. A.19.

In the first half of 1971 a *double bottom* pattern can clearly be seen. The first bottom was at 105p, and the second at 107p. The price subsequently rose to 182p so that the double bottom was an indication of a substantial

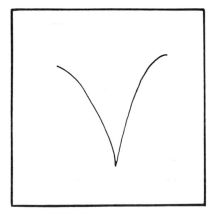

Figure A.17. 'V' bottom.

Figure A.18. Saucer bottom.

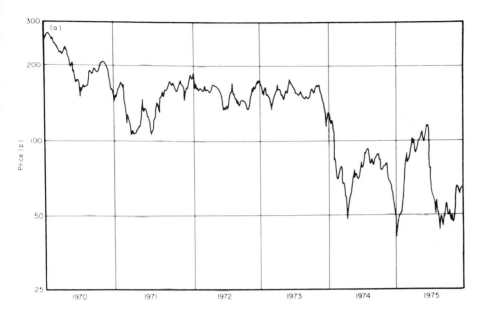

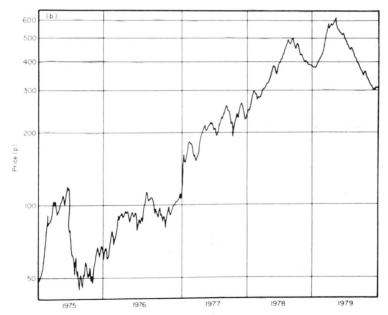

Figure A.19. Share price of John Brown (a) from 1970 to 1975, (b) from 1975 to 1979 (prices are on a logarithmic scale).

price rise in a share which had been falling throughout the previous year. Throughout 1972 and 1973 the price fell several times to a *support level* of 130p and bounced up several times to a *resistance level* of about 175p. Once the support level was penetrated in late 1973 the price fell drastically to a low of 42p. A large *inverted head and shoulders* can be seen taking the two years 1974 and 1975 for its completion. A rise above the inverted neckline in 1976 saw the price rise up to nearly 600p in 1979. The price oscillations during 1977 and 1978 are part of a *curved uptrend* line.

In the chart of Babcock & Wilcox over the past 10 years (Fig. 11.3) a number of features can again be distinguished. A long *uptrend line* continued from mid 1970 until 1973. A *rounded top* formation is apparent during 1973 which eventually led to a closely spaced double bottom in late 1974. This was followed by a very substantial rise through 1975 and 1976. A good illustration of an *uptrend channel* can be seen during 1977.

These two examples serve to illustrate quite well the various types of pattern we have been discussing in this chapter. Of course we could present the chart of virtually any share price and find similar examples. We could also give examples to show that such patterns are not always indications of the future course of events, but it can be left to the reader to find those points in the John Brown and Babcock & Wilcox charts where a reliance on the pattern could have led to disaster. Remember we are working here with the benefit of hindsight; but to put yourself in the position as it would have been at the time, it would be instructive to cover the chart with a sheet of paper, and then slowly move it to the right so that the share price then unravels. Now test yourself by asking yourself frequently what investment decision you would take based upon what you can see up to that point. Hopefully this exercise will have a sobering effect upon any thoughts you might hold that charts of share prices offer a quick way to riches. We can but reiterate our statement at the beginning of this chapter—read patterns in conjunction with all the other signals and information available to you!

Appendix B

Microcomputers and the Smaller Investor

The sales of microcomputers in the UK over the last few years have risen dramatically, and can expect to rise at an ever increasing rate in the immediate future. There are two main reasons for this; firstly, the relatively low cost of these—from just under £100 for a 64K computer which can be plugged into the TV for displaying input and output, to about £3000 for a typical small business system with disk storage and printer—and, secondly, the saving in time and improvement in accuracy to be obtained in complex calculations and book-keeping, stock control, invoicing, payroll etc. The micro is ideal for repetitive calculations and for record-keeping and storage. It will have become apparent throughout the course of this book that these aspects have formed the very basis of our investment strategy. Besides this, the microcomputer can be used to keep track of the results of our investments, in the sense that it can record our purchases and sales, the dividends we have received, when dividends are due, and calculate our capital gains (losses?) for tax purposes at the end of each tax year. Commercial programs are available for these tasks (see address in Appendix E).

As with any other sphere of activity, a lot of jargon is associated with microcomputers, such as 'floppy disks', serial interfaces, modems, '32K' etc., and hence it is worthwhile cutting through this before proceeding further.

The 'memory' of a computer is expressed Kbytes, meaning thousands of bytes. An 8K computer therefore has a memory capacity of about 8000 bytes. In fact, because computers are based on binary numbers, such a computer would have $2^{13} = 8192$ bytes of memory, but this is always called '8K'. Although not strictly correct, we can define a byte as a character, such as 1, or A, or % or +; this enables us to present a microcomputer as a device which can hold a large number of characters in its memory. A set of instructions will occupy some of the memory. This set of instructions is called a program. The rest of the memory is free to store the results of its calculations, or to store numbers of letters input from the keyboard, or to store data read in from a storage device such as a floppy disk or cassette tape. The results of carrying out the instructions can be displayed on a TV screen, or VDU (visual display unit), printed out by a printer, or stored on disk etc. for access at a later date.

The vast majority of microcomputers are programmed in a language called BASIC, which unfortunately is not quite standard between computers. A program writen for a BBC micro would require changes to run on an Apple, and other modifications to run on an Apricot. However, these changes are usually relatively trivial, and the great advantage of BASIC is that it is easy to learn. Most local higher education and adult education centres now run short day or evening courses on BASIC programming.

Since moving averages have been the prime consideration in this book, a BASIC program to run on an Apple computer and calculate moving averages of any time span up to 1000 weeks is given in Table A.1. Also shown is some of the printout for a 5-week moving average. Although the program is stored on a floppy disk and can be run by entering RUN and the name of the program, any data for weekly prices which is entered from the keyboard is lost once the computer is shut off or another program is run. The program in Table A.2 however does not suffer from this disadvantage. The weekly data is stored in the program, and the advantage is that any moving average can be calculated without the laborious tasks of re-entering the prices. The data list can also be scanned for errors before the program is finally saved on disk.

An even better way of carrying out this operation is to have the price data stored in a named file. The name of the file, which can be the same as the share name, is then requested by the program, which reads it and carries out the calculations. Each week a master program requests that week's closing prices of say 100 shares that you are following, and uses this to update each individual share file. A program to carry out all the tasks and calculations summarized in Chapter 8 is now available commercially (Appendix E). This program automatically tells the investor when to buy, what to buy and when to sell! The only operation is to enter the FT Index each week, the data for the 200 most volatile shares once at some point in the falling market, and from then on enter the weekly prices of shares which it has told you to buy. Could anything be simpler?

Table A.1. Simple program to calculate moving averages

```
]LIST

5      P = 0
10     DIM A (1000)
20     IINPUT "NUMBER OF POINTS OF MOVING AVERAGE"; N
25     FOR I = 1 TO N
30     INPUT "ENTER X:"; X
45     P = P + X
50     A(I) = X
60     NEXT I
70     PRINT "X = "; X, "AVGE = "; P/N
80     INPUT "ENTER X: "; X
83     IF X = − 1 THEN 200
85     P = P + X − A(1)
90     PRINT "X = "; X, "AVGE = "; P/N
100    FOR J = 2 TO N
110    A(J − 1) = A(J)
130    NEXT J
140    A(N) = X
170    GOTO 80
200    END

]
```

```
 RUN
NUMBER OF POINTS OF MOVING AVERAGE 5
ENTER X: 12
ENTER X: 13
ENTER X: 14
ENTER X: 15
ENTER X: 16
X = 16              AVGE = 14
ENTER X: 15
X = 15              AVGE = 14.6
ENTER X: 14
X = 14              AVGE = 14.8
ENTER X: 17
X = 17              AVGE = 15.4
ENTER X: 18
X = 18              AVGE = 16
ENTER X: 18
X = 18              AVGE = 16.4
ENTER X: 19
X = 19              AVGE = 17.2
ENTER X: − 1

]
```

Table A.2. Program for retaining weekly prices and printing a moving average of the weekly data

LIST

```
10      DIM A(1000)
20      DIM B(1000)
200     FOR I = 1 TO 1000
210     READ D
220     IF D = 0 THEN 210
225     IF D = 99999 THEN 1000
230     A(I) = D
240     NEXT I
1000    INPUT "NO. OF POINTS OF AVERAGE < ODD NO. > "; C
1005    PRINT "BABCOCK INTERNATIONAL"; C; "WEEK MOVING AVERAGE"
1006    PRINT : PRINT
1007    PRINT "WEEK NUMBER PRICE MOVING AVERAGE"
1010    D = 0
1020    X = 1
1030    Z = 0
1040    FOR N = X TO(C + X − 1)
1050    IF A(N) = 0 THEN 9999
1060    Z = Z + A(N)
1070    NEXT N
1080    LET D = D + 1
1090    B(D + (C − 1)/2) = Z/C
1095    PRINT D,A (D), (INT(B(D) * 10))/10
1110    X = X + 1
1120    GOTO 1030
4910    REM 1970 DATA
4912    DATA    48,50,52,49,48,48,51,47,47,47,49,48,51,51,49,47,44,51
4914    DATA    51,50,46,42,45,49,43,48,48,49,49,50,51,51,51,51,50,49
4916    DATA    50,53,51,51,50,52,51,49,52,50,51,50,50,50,50,51,0,0
4920    REM 1971 DATA
4922    DATA    53,55,57,57,56,55,53,53,52,53,54,53,53,55,53,56,57,59
4924    DATA    58,61,64,61,60,60,58,57,59,63,63,62,61,61,60,62,62,62
4926    DATA    62,61,62,59,63,63,61,60,61,62,63,63,66,64,65,67,70,0
4930    REM 1972 DATA
4932    DATA    68,70,67,69,71,75,77,81,80,77,80,84,88,87,94,92,94,91
4934    DATA    90,88,87,81,80,79,80,78,82,78,83,82,89,84,81,79,78,84
4936    DATA    80,81,85,91,87,85,83,86,83,83,83,83,91,100,95,95,0,0
4940    REM 1973 DATA
4942    DATA    93,94,91,86,88,90,88,88,83,85,85,88,91,96,96,96,98,94
4944    DATA    94,98,98,98,94,94,98,94,96,94,96,94,96,98,101,99,96,94
4946    DATA    93,86,88,90,91,88,91,91,88,83,80,70,67,59,66,70,0,0
4950    REM 1974 DATA
4952    DATA    69,66,67,61,61,62,61,61,60,55,55,50,37,51,56,60,58,56
4954    DATA    53,55,55,53,55,46,43,42,45,50,51,46,42,38,38,43,53,43
4956    DATA    38,37,34,34,35,35,37,34,32,30,26,26,27,29,30,29,0,0
4960    REM 1975 DATA
4962    DATA    25,25,28,28,30,34,36,38,40,40,40,37,39,50,54,63,60,60
4964    DATA    60,68,69,69,69,68,68,63,63,61,60,59,54,53,59,65,70,70
4966    DATA    70,77,68,68,67,66,69,70,71,70,69,66,70,69,70,69,0,0
4970    REM 1976 DATA
4972    DATA    73,74,74,76,79,80,77,72,77,75,76,77,80,80,80,88,85,89
4974    DATA    89,88,89,81,79,81,84,80,83,80,84,82,79,77,75,70,65,66
```

Table A.2. *(cont'd)*

```
4976   DATA   71,67,69,62,62,58,53,55,60,60,60,57,55,60,59,61,61,0
4980   REM 1977 DATA
4982   DATA   76,79,75,78,80,76,77,77,74,77,77,80,81,79,85,85,88,90
       4984   DATA   92,92,104,106,102,104,102,104,99,103,98,96,110,110,
       118,125,125,140
4986   DATA   130,120,120,120,120,120,120,106,108,107,105,116,114,
       114,114,116,0,0
4990   REM 1978 DATA
4992   DATA   116,112,112,113,113,115,112,109,109,116,111,113,
       113,116,117,114,123,128
4994   DATA   132,131,130,130,130,133,127,129,127,132,132,137,
       140,146,141,142,138,137
4996   DATA   148,148,149,151,152,166,157,152,146,149,154,162,162,
       158,153,147,0,0
5000   REM 1979 DATA
5002   DATA   151,151,155,151,152,143,145,150,160,169,169,172,
       169,166,174,180,192,198
5004   DATA   184,175,181,181,177,155,151,161,166,164,166,158,
       149,150,154,146,147,140
5006   DATA   131,120,125,128,122,119,115,109,106,109,108,106,101,
       111,108,104,0,0
5010   REM 1980 DATA
5012   DATA   100,105,112,108,99,98,101,99,107,106,102,96,94,93,98,99,
       93,99
6000   DATA   99999
9999   END
```

]

Appendix C

Glossary of Stock Exchange Terms

Account: the period into which the Stock Exchange transactions are divided (usually 2 weeks, sometimes 3 weeks).

After-hours dealings: dealings between members' offices after 3.30 p.m. when the Stock Exchange officially closes.

Arbitrage: the taking advantage of the different prices in different markets by buying in one market and selling in the other.

Averaging: buying more securities on a fall or selling more on a rise, so as to level out the price of bull or bear transactions.

Bargain: a sale or a purchase between a jobber and a broker.

Bear: one who sells securities not owned by himself in the expectation that they can be bought again at a lower price before delivery is due.

Bid: when there are more buyers than sellers, a price may be quoted as 'bid'.

Blue chip: a company which may be regarded as a fairly safe investment, usually one which is quite large and well established.

Broken amount: an odd amount, which is not a usual market quantity. A seller may have to accept less than the market price, as the costs of transfer are proportionately more than for even amounts.

Bull: one who buys securities in the expectation that they will rise in price. If his optimism is on the wane, and he is ready to take a loss, he is known as a 'stale bull'.

Call option: the right to buy shares after the purchase of a call option.

Calls: the amounts which may be still payable after allotment in order that the securities may be fully paid. Over a period of a few months there may be one or two, or more calls. Forfeiture of the stock may result in the failure to meet them.

Cash settlement: payment is due on the following day, unlike normal Stock

Exchange Account transactions for settlement. Gilt-edged securities are normally paid for in this way.

Close price: a narrow margin between the bid price and the offered price.

Closing prices: the prices at the official close of the House, at 3.30 p.m. and business transacted after this close is at 'after-hours' prices.

Contango: a rate of interest paid for carrying over a transaction from one account to another.

Coupon: the warrant, which usually has pages of coupons attached, which must be presented before collection of interest or dividends on bearer securities. The 'Talon' the last item on the old sheet, must be presented before obtaining new pages of coupons.

Cum: means 'with'. If a price is quoted 'cum' it includes any recently declared dividend, a scrip issue, rights or any other distribution.

Difference: the balance due to or by a client when buying or selling a security during a stock exchange account.

Discount: the amount, below its par or paid-up value, by which a security is quoted, i.e. a 50p share, paid-up to 25p, is quoted at 22½p, standing at a discount of 2½p.

Dollar stocks: American and Canadian stocks and shares.

Dollar premium: the premium beyond the usual exchange rate paid for 'investment dollars', which have to be bought in order to pay for American, Canadian and other hard currency stocks.

Equity: ordinary shares, which normally take most of the profits and all the risks. The equity-holders retain what is left after the demands of any other classes of capital have been met.

Ex: means 'without'. A price quoted 'ex', excludes dividends recently declared, scrip issue, rights or any other distribution.

Free: without stamp and fee, which means that these expenses are paid by the seller, usually on the sale of small lot of securities. It also applies when transacting new securities in allotment letter form, free of stamp duty until they have to be registered.

Funds: British Government stocks (also known as 'gilt-edged').

Gilt-edged: British Government and other fixed-interest securities.

Instalment: new issues of securities are often paid for over a period of time, in application and allotment money, followed by one or more instalments.

Interim dividend: dividend payments may be spread over the year by distribution of an interim, or more than one interim, followed by final payment at the end of the year.

Jobber's turn: the difference between the buying and selling prices at which a jobber is ready to deal. If the price is 85–87p the turn is 2p. When calculating the cost of buying and selling this should be taken into account.

Kaffirs: South African mining and related shares.

Limit: a broker can be 'limited' by his client to buying at a stated maximum price or selling at a stated minimum price.

Limited market: when it is difficult to buy or sell, because of shortage of stock for example, one or more securities are described as a limited market.

Lists closed: application lists for public issues and offers for sale are for a certain time. Lists are closed when the time expires or the offer is fully subscribed.

Long: anyone who holds an amount of a certain stock.

Longs: government and similar stocks with repayment dates more than 15 years in the future.

Making a price: when a price is quoted or 'made' by a jobber, he is about to buy at the lower price and sell at the higher price, in a reasonable quantity.

Marketable amount: the number of shares or stocks which would be reasonable for a jobber to deal with, when he has quoted a price.

Marking: details or the price at which brokers and jobbers transact a bargain, is entered on a marking slip, which is used for recording business done in the Official List.

Mediums: government and similar stocks with repayment dates varying between 5 and 15 years.

Moneystocks: very short-dated gilt-edged or any other securities which fall due for repayment at a certain date in the very near future.

Name ticket: the form which states the registration details on the purchase of securities, which the broker who is buying must give to the seller.

New time: purchases or sales in one account for settlement in the next. This type of deal can be done during the last 2 days of the old account.

Nominal: when a jobber quotes a price, but is not prepared to deal, the price is known as nominal and is simply an *indication* of the price.

NTP: this stands for 'not to press' and means that the buyer has an agreement with the jobber not to press for delivery if this delayed beyond the usual time.

Offered: there are usually more sellers than buyers when a price is so much 'offered'.

One way: 'one way only' means that a jobber cannot deal both ways, but can only bid for or offer stock.

Opening prices: the prices quoted by the Stock Exchange every day, at the official opening for business.

Pitch: the place where one would find a jobber on the floor of the House.

Position: a jobber has a position when he is a 'bull' (holding stock) or is a 'bear' (short of stock).

Premium: a security is at a premium when the price is greater than its paid-up or par value.

Put and call option: the right to buy or sell shares under an option.

Put option: the right to sell shares after the purchase of a put option.

Renunciation: shareholders are usually given the opportunity of selling their rights, given to them by a company, if they do not want to take up the offer. Their rights are then 'renounced' to a buyer.

Scrip issue: a capitalization of reserves and retained profits in the form of a 'free' issue of shares.

Settlement: payment for securities is either for cash, on the day after purchase or sale, or account usually days after the end of the 2- or 3-weekly account.

Short: when stock which is not owned has been sold, one is known to be short.

Shorts: gilt-edged stocks due for repayment within 5 years.

Shunter: a broker who deals between London and other United Kingdom stock exchanges with securities which are quoted in both.

Small: when the price made to a broker by a jobber is for less than a usual market quantity of stocks or shares.

Stag: one who applies for new issues and sells his allotment at the beginning of dealings, at a profit or loss.

To open: an announcement that the order is to buy or sell, or to get someone else to 'open'.

Touch: the nearest price quoted between the jobbers, or the highest price bid by one, and the lowest offered by another.

Undated: Government and other stocks which have no fixed dates for their repayment. Sometimes known as 'irredeemables'.

Unquoted: Securities which do not appear in the Official List or monthly supplement. Transactions in these can be carried out under Rule 163 (1)(e).

Wide price: a greater than usual difference between bid and offered prices.

Appendix D

The Companies in the FTSE-100 Index

Allied Lyons
Associated British Foods
Associated Dairies
BAT Industries
BICC
BOC Group
BPB International
BTR
Barclays Bank
Bass
Beecham Group
S. W. Berisford
Blue Circle Industries
Boots
British & Commonwealth
British Aerospace
British Electric Traction
British Home Stores
British Petroleum
Britoil
British Telecom
Burton Group
Cable & Wireless
Cadbury Schweppes
Rothschild J. Holdings
Commercial Union

Consolidated Gold Fields
Courtaulds
Dalgety
Distillers
Dowty Group
English China Clays
Exco International
Ferranti
Fisons
General Accident
GEC
Glaxo
Globe Investment Trust
Granada Group
Grand Metropolitan
Great Universal Stores
Guardian Royal Exchange
   Assurance
GKN
Hambro Life Assurance
Hammerson Property
Hanson Trust
Harrisons & Crosfield
Hawker Siddeley
House of Fraser
Imperial Chemical Industries

Imperial Continental Gas
Imperial Group
Johnson Matthey
Ladbroke Group
Land Securities
Legal & General
Lloyds Bank
Lonrho
MEPC
Marks & Spencer
Midland Bank
National Westminster Bank
Northern Foods
P & O
S. Pearson
Pilkington Brothers
Plessey
Prudential
RMC Group
Racal Electronics
Rank Organisation
Reckitt & Colman
Redland
Reed International
Reuters

Rio Tinto Zinc
Rowntree Mackintosh
Royal Bank of Scotland
Royal Insurance
Sainsbury
Sears Holdings
Sedgwick
Shell Transport & Trading
Smith and Nephew
Standard Chartered Bank
Standard Telephones & Cables
Sun Alliance & London Assurance
Sunlife Assurance Society
Thorn EMI
Tarmac
Tesco
Trafalgar House
Trusthouse Forte
Ultramar
Unilever
United Biscuits
Whitbread
Willis Faber
Woolworth

Appendix E

Useful Information

Addresses
1. For lists of brokers:
   The Secretary
   The Stock Exchange
   London EC2
2. For consultancy, monthly newsletter and microcomputer software:
   Brian Millard Investment Services,
   16 Queensgate
   Bramhall
   Stockport
   Cheshire SK7 1JT
   Tel: 061 439 3926
3. For printed share price data:
   Eflow Text
   53 Cambridge Street
   Aylesbury
   Bucks. HP20 1RP
   Tel: 0296 37652

Newspapers and periodicals
1. *Financial Times*, published Monday–Saturday (Monday's issue gives month for dividends of quoted shares)
2. *Investors Chronicle*, published weekly
3. *What investment?*, published monthly
4. For a quick catch-up on the weeks events:
   Sunday Times, business news section
   Observer, business news section
   Sunday Telegraph, business news section

5. Most daily newspapers carry at least a half-page of business comment and share prices.
6. For United States markets, the *Wall Street Journal* is now obtainable in London.

The Effect of the 1986 Budget on the Small Investor

The Chancellor, in his 1986 Budget introduced several measures which make investment in stocks and shares even more attractive to the small private investor. The cost of buying shares has been reduced because of a lowering of stamp duty, the rules relating to traditional employee share schemes have been relaxed, and the Chancellor will be bringing in Personal Equity Plans for the regular investor.

Stamp Duty

The rate of stamp duty on share purchases will be reduced to 0.5% from 27 October 1986, although matching transactions which were previously exempted from stamp duty if they occurred within the same Stock Exchange account will now become liable.

Employee Share Schemes

In future more companies will be able to set up approved schemes because the Inland Revenue are viewing compulsory buy-back clauses in a more relaxed way. Workers' co-operatives will also be able to introduce profit-sharing schemes using redeemable shares.

Personal Equity Plans

These plans will be allowed from 1 January 1987, and represent a radical departure from the thinking of previous Chancellors. The proceeds on investments of up to £200 per month are treated as tax free, both from the dividends and the capital gains aspect. Naturally in the initial years, dividends are likely to be modest, so the income tax saving may be of the order of £50 or so. Any capital gains made are tax free, and are in addition to the current capital gains allowance of £6300.

The value of the plan lies in creating a climate where regular investment in shares is seen to be an integral part of the savings and investment scene. The real tax advantages may take some years to become apparent, when a valuable holding has been built up. The scheme is particularly appropriate for those investors who follow the philosophy of Chapter 9 of this book, where the principle of cost averaging is applied.